What I Wish I Had Known 25 Years Ago

Sherman Owens

ISBN: 1-931600-42-2
Copyright © 2003 Sherman Owens
8200 Bee Ridge Road
Sarasota, Florida 34241

Published by
Leadership Publishing

Printed in the United States of America.
All rights reserved under International Copyright Law.

Contents and/or cover may not be reproduced in whole or in part in any form without the express written consent of the Publisher.

TABLE OF CONTENTS

Anointing	1
Unlearning	5
Reality	7
Timing	11
Law of the Farm	15
Weaknesses	19
Haste	23
Substance	27
Staff	29
Battles	33
Differences	37
Wisdom	39
No	43
Disloyalty	45
Diaries and Journals	47
Mentorship	49
Respond	51
Savings	53
Importance	55
Relationships	57
Price Tags	59
Family	61
Risks	65
Trust	69
Emotions	73
Cost	75
Extremes	77

Requests	79
The Library	81
Relax	83
Perception	85
Criticism	87
Humor	91
Hurts	93
Health	95
Action	99
Fashion	101
Life Stages	105
Confrontation	107
Prudence	111
Masks	115
Teamwork	117
Change	119

WISDOM HONOR ROLL

To my partners who believe in wisdom and me... You made this book "What I Wish I Had Known 25 Years Ago" possible. When we stand before God's throne it will be worth it all as we hear His approval, "well done". I have asked God to multiply the precious seed which you have sown back to your life 100-fold just as He has promised in Mark 10:30.

Clarence & Bobbi Addy
Gwen Atkins
Soloman Barnes
Phil & Karen Bender
Joseph Bisconti
Bret Bottomley
Andrea Buckmaster
Duane & Maria Buckmaster,
Kirk & Sheila Carothers
Frank & Janet Cryan
Victoria Devine
Joseph, Heather & Joey Devineaux
Bob & Karen Dring
Peggy Dudeck
Sharlene Graham
Sarah Gulotta
Yolanda Hammond
Leora Hand
Adam, Donna, Jon & Dan Hernandez
Roger & Laurie Hill
Tracy & Velma Jackson
Mel & Martha Kaufman

Wisdom Honor Roll (continued)

Roger Kaufman
Tom & Sue Kema
Sally Kerr
Bernard & Thetu Kisholyian
Ron & Donna Kutinsky
Renford & Barbara Laidlaw
Carol Lavoie
Trisha Megar
Maureen Morgan
Lloyd Myers
Pat Nixon
Diane Owens
Debi Packard
Robert & BettyAnne Peacock
Pamella Perkins
Kevin, Vedda & Chris Peters
David & Maria Polimeni
Jesse & Pat Pryor
Rajin & Kavita Ramsaran
Deanna Robinson
Sheila Roby
Paul & Clauda Schlimgen
Annette Schmidt
David & Susie Shue
Don & Mary Sprague
Bruce & Charlene Spranger
Ann St. George
Amy Swedberg
Moody & Susan Whiddon
Arthur & Loreda Williams

Introduction

There are many things you learn best by living them. I wouldn't have admitted that over 23 years ago when I started the ministry. At that time I didn't have a lot of experience. I just believed in standing on the Word of God. I believed the Word of God was all I needed. Of course it was. But I needed to *experience* the Word.

I've discovered that there are some things you learn best by living them. Some things you understand better once it happens to you. Ecclesiastes 1:16 says, "My heart has experienced great wisdom." Limited experiences create a limited life! There is no bad experience. Every experience is of value; look for the value in it. Learn from it.

The Wisdom of Experience

Wisdom is experienced. <u>It's not something you recite. It's not something you simply store in your memory</u>. Solomon talked about that wisdom. Most of it is recorded in the book of Proverbs.

You **hear** from teaching. You **learn** by living. Over 20 years of pastoring at Victory Christian Family Center has taught me a lot of things about people.

Knowledge comes by hearing, and **wisdom** comes by observation **and** by living. You **hear** knowledge. You **see** wisdom. There are things that you learn from observation. There are things you learn through touch. There are things you learn through sight and sound. There are things you learn through miracles and mistakes. There are things you learn through your victories.

Think. Learning is much more than taking in information. It's acting on the information. It's **unlearning**. It's **forgiving**. It's **changing**. It becomes **real** once you've done it. It's like driving a car. You can learn all about the car, but once you get in that car, and you push the clutch pedal, put it into gear, and push that gas pedal, then it becomes real to you. Now you really know how to drive; you don't just know about driving.

There's a kind of information you get **in** school, and then there's the kind of information you get **after** school. Put those two together and I believe you'll find wisdom. I would not trust someone if everything he knew, he learned from a book. I want to trust someone who has been through it. They fought for the information they have given me. The information your mentor will give you was won on the battlefield. It was probably won on the front lines. It's valuable information that you cannot trade for anything else.

There's a lot of information that you know after you live 50 or 60 years that didn't come from formulas or the classroom. It came through experience. You actually saw it happen. You actually walked through it. **Hindsight** can be great. **Foresight** is greater. But **insight** is the greatest. You need all three:
- **Hindsight**
- **Foresight**
- **Insight**

Between said and done is experience. There's a time gap there. What makes you an expert? Mistakes make you an expert. Failures make you an expert. A man who's had a tiger by the tail can tell you a few things about the tiger that no one else can.

In another translation, Ecclesiastes 1:16 says, "My heart has understood great wisdom." The word "**understood**" is used for the word "**experienced.**" My heart has **experienced** great wisdom. **Experience is something you understand**. You read the Bible and you say, "Now I see it." Then you apply it to your life. In the eighth chapter of Jeremiah, Israel refused to learn from their mistakes. It cost them everything they had. There is one thing worse than hardness of heart, and that is softness of head.

There are some experiences you don't want to learn firsthand. It's better to let the rattlesnake bite the other fellow. I'll tell you there are some things you want to learn from your mentor, or from someone else so that you don't have to go through it yourself. You don't want the pain. You don't want the heartache. The more you can learn from someone else's experience, the better.

Still, there are some things you are going to have to go through to learn. You're going to have to apply it. A man will never really know how to be a son until he becomes a father. When you become a father, you realize some of the mistakes you made as a son.

The Value of Hindsight

Ecclesiastes 7:14 says, "In the day of prosperity be joyful." We're to be happy or joyful in the day of prosperity. Then it says, "But in the day of adversity consider." That's the day you need to stop, think and consider. Ask yourself, "How did I get in this mess? What happened? Where did I make a mistake? Did I make a mistake, or is this a natural cause of nature?"

I think about Abraham. Wouldn't it have been something if Abraham would've had some wisdom before he had the good idea. He and Sarah had this good idea of helping God out by Abraham jumping in the tent with Hagar. We know that a boy called Ishmael was birthed out of that. The Jews and Arabs are still fighting today because Abraham didn't have wisdom before he had the good idea.

What if Moses had wisdom before he had the idea of killing that Egyptian? As you look at all the Bible heroes, you see there are times in their lives when they were acting in outright stupidity. I mean, they were just oozing with ignorance.

If Abraham had not gotten in that tent with Hagar, there would be no Ishmael. The Arabs and the Jews would not be fighting today. All of our eyes are turned towards Israel, that little old itty-bitty thumbprint of a nation. There are many, many nations that are much larger, but you never hear of them. If someone told you the names of those nations, you would say, "I have never heard of those nations." It's been that way because the Bible says all eyes will be on Israel in the last days. You hear the presidents trying to bring peace to Israel. You hear them saying, "We've got peace. We've got peace." They're all hugging each other and shaking each other's hands, "Oh there's peace at last!" But how long does it last? A week or two, and they're fighting again.

Joseph should have had wisdom before he announced his dream.

Confessing dreams can cause crisis. They will cause a crisis in your life, believe me, but nothing is going to happen until you stand up and confess your dreams.

Joseph confessed his dream, and he confessed it to the wrong people. He ended up in a pit. He made a mistake. He couldn't contain it. If you can contain it, it is not really a dream. I am not saying that he shouldn't have told his dream, but he would have been wise if he hadn't told his parents that they were going to bow down and serve him one day.

What if David would have had wisdom before he met Bathsheba? Think about that. He was a great man of wisdom, but he just fell into stupidity. He was at home on his roof, just walking around, and he saw Bathsheba. We know the end of that story. It cost him a son. Then it cost him another son. Tragedy was brought to his life. That was when he wrote most of the Psalms. That's how he repented and became a man after God's own heart.

Look at Samson. What if he would have had some wisdom before he went into the tent with that woman Delilah? If only these men had wisdom **before** their plans. They needed wisdom before their plans. They had plans, but they were lousy plans. Wisdom before the plan...I want wisdom before the plan. If they would've had wisdom, we wouldn't be suffering some of the things we are today.

Intelligence Isn't Enough

Believe me, Satan's goal is to keep you ignorant. Ignorance isn't that you don't know anything. You can know much more than I know and still be ignorant. His goal is not to make you sin, because you can repent. Repentance solves sinning. His goal is not to make you fall, because God said He'd pick you up. His goal is to keep you ignorant, or to keep you lacking wisdom. What is wisdom? It is the law of God applied. It's the mind of God applied to your situation. That's believing. You're not really Bible believing until you apply the law of God to your situation.

I think of people who need to give their hearts to Christ. It's more than just a confession. When it turns into action, it really counts before God. When you're giving your life to God, you're giving your actions and your decisions to God. That's believing. That's really faith. The only sin that cannot be forgiven is not acting on God's Word. That's called unbelief. God knows everything. He doesn't change, but He does move. You change once you have the Mover on the inside of you.

I've always been concerned about the fact that God turned certain people over to their own ways. He seemed to make them more ignorant than they were. Romans 1:28 says, "And even as they did not like to retain God in their knowledge...."

I thought about that. It doesn't mean they didn't know anything. They could've been very intelligent and still have been ignorant. It says, "They did not want to bring God into their knowledge." It means they ignored God. The dictionary calls this "willful blindness." They were willfully blinded. They refused to bring God into the picture.

It's the same today. We've got a lot of intelligent people in our government. You do have to be pretty smart to do some of the things in government, but these people refuse to acknowledge God in their actions. They separate church and state.

The word "ignore" means to refuse to notice. They refused to notice God. Even as people did not like to retain God in their knowledge, and God gave them over to a reprobate mind. Why did God give them over? Because they refused to acknowledge Him as God. They refused to acknowledge His ways. They did it willfully. They thought they had a better way.

There are many judgments that come from experience. Our good judgment comes from experience. Bad judgment comes from lack of experience. Education is what you get from reading the small print. Experience is what you get from not reading the small print. We need to read the small print. Problems occur when you fail to read the small print.

Failure Isn't Fatal

Failure is not having a problem. Failure is having the same problem this year that you had last year. When you see someone have the same problem over and over again, you see a failure.

I have friends and every time I see them they have the same problem. We all have friends like that. It's always the same problem. What they're doing is baby-sitting a problem. It's the same problem year after year. They haven't seen the real problem yet. When they see the real problem, it can be solved. They're not seeing the problem; they are seeing what the problem is creating. When they get to the root of the problem, they will be able to take care of it.

So many times the problem is solved once we see the real problem, but seeing the source of the problem too late doesn't help. Experience gives wisdom to some, and it gives grief to others. A wise man makes a ladder out of his experience. A foolish man makes a grave out of his experience.

Wisdom from experience builds character. Having experience is not a bad thing. Not learning from the experience is a bad thing. I believe that wisdom from experience builds character. In Romans 5:3 Paul says, "We glory in tribulation."

Why would Paul say, "I give glory to God in my tribulations?" How could he say that? He knew something. He continues saying, "Knowing that tribulation produces perseverance, and perseverance, character." There's no character without perseverance.

What I Wish I Had Known 25 Years Ago...

I want to share with you some things that I've learned in the last 25 years through experience. These are some things I wish someone would have told me 25 years ago. It's powerful to me. It is not in a specific order. These are things that I've learned through my experience. It's my list, not your list. I keep adding to this list, so it is not complete.

Understand this truth. The **years** will teach you what the **days** won't teach you. We remember **moments**, not **years**. Just have patience, and be comfortable. Just learn everything you can. Sometimes you think you're not changing, but you will find out that over a period of time you are. The years will teach you what the days will not teach you. It just happens over a period of time.

There are 43 principles that I wish I would have known 25 years ago when I started in the ministry. I won't spend a lot of time on each one of them, but I will look in my rear view mirror and share some things I wish I would have known when I started out in the ministry.

I've experienced these things, and one day I began to make a list. I just kept adding to it, and adding to it. Then I said, "I need to minister this, because it's pretty good."

I've heard other ministers, like Mike Murdock, talk about what they wished they could know if they started their lives over again. So, I started looking at my life. Here's what I came up with. If only I had known then what I know now...

Chapter 1

Anointing

I wish I had known that I needed more than the anointing. When I started Victory, I thought, "All I need is the anointing. It will solve all my problems." I didn't think I needed anything else. My prayer was, "God, just anoint me. Just touch me."

Anointing will start a ministry, but wisdom will see it through to the end.

You must have the anointing. I was partially right. If you don't have the anointing, what you're doing is not worth anything. If you don't have the anointing, you don't have God's stamp of approval. You'd better have the anointing, but you can't stop there. Anointing will get you where God wants to take you, but wisdom will keep you there.

I began to see that a man can be dumb and still have the anointing. There are plenty of people with God's anointing who, at times, act like idiots. We see examples throughout the Bible. God even anointed a donkey once. I Samuel 15:17 says, "Saul was anointed, but he had no wisdom." He was the anointed king of Israel, but he lost it all. There are four places in the book of Judges where the Spirit of the Lord moved upon Samson. Yet Samson never did anything to bring freedom to his people. He had the anointing, but he didn't do anything with it. He didn't have any wisdom. Even Judas, the one who betrayed Jesus, was anointed. Did you know that Judas was just like all the other disciples? He worked miracles. Then he went and sold Jesus for 30 pieces of silver. David, Abraham, Joshua, Joseph, Moses, and Solomon were all anointed, but they each had seasons in their lives when they made terrible mistakes. It was not lack of anointing, but lack of wisdom, which deterred them from achieving all they could for God.

Satan was anointed. He made the decision to take over while he was under the anointing of God. The anointing impressed him. People were following him. He was evidently the head of praise and worship. He was the lead singer. He was God's right hand man, and he still decided to try to take over. Imagine that! He rebelled and attempted to overthrow God while he was under the Lord's anointing and ministering in His presence.

I don't fully understand it, but there are some anointed men of God who are not serving in the ministry today. There is a man who worked some of the greatest miracles ever seen. His name is well known, but he died of AIDS. Only two or three people went to his funeral. This man would fill up stadiums. He was known as the "Miracle Worker," but he died a lonely, depressing death. He needed more than just the anointing.

Now, Jesus was anointed, and He grew in wisdom. He grew in wisdom before He used His anointing. He was anointed at 12, 13, 14, and 15 years old, but He was 30 years old before He worked a miracle. He didn't use the anointing until He had experience.

Anointing and wisdom through experience can change the world.

I WISH I HAD KNOWN THAT BACK THEN.

Chapter 2

Unlearning

If only I had known that it is impossible to learn what you think you already know. It took me years to learn these principles I am sharing now. One of the reasons it took so long is this: when I started the ministry, I thought I had it all. Allow me to explain. I knew I didn't know it all, but I thought I knew where all the answers were. I thought Tulsa had it all.

I remember going through that phase. Everything was Tulsa and Rhema. They had it all. I thought, "Just get the anointing, get faith, and that's all you'll ever need." I was wrong. Don't misunderstand me. I am a Rhema fan. I am still a Tulsa fan. That hasn't changed. It's just that now I realize they don't have ALL the answers.

I began to see that no one person has it all. I began to feel that I needed to know about some other things that didn't come out of Tulsa. I began to search. I went outside of the walls I had put up. I began to learn some things about leadership. I found out that I had developed my "Faith" side. I had developed my "Gifts of the Spirit" side, my "Who I am in Christ" side, and my "Abundance" side, but when it came to leadership, I had no knowledge whatsoever. I began to see that wisdom is like a house. It has different rooms, and each room has a different view. It doesn't mean that you are to embrace all those different views, but you should at least look at them. I wouldn't go to relax and sit in front of the window where I can see all my trashcans lined up, but I surely do need to know where they are.

I said I had built walls, and I had to go outside of them. Don't put walls around your spiritual knowledge or faith. Remember what Paul said to the Thessalonians: "Test everything, and hold on to the good." With God's wisdom, you'll have to spit some things out, swallow some others, and take years to digest some others. Some things you will chew, and chew, and chew. It may take your whole lifetime.

As you grow in wisdom, you'll grow in the knowledge that there is so much you don't know. That's why wisdom should never puff you up or make you think you are someone you're not. The farther you sail out into the ocean, the more you know how large the ocean really is. You'll learn and you'll realize there is so much more to learn. There is so much to know. Start there today.

I WISH I HAD KNOWN THAT BACK THEN.

Chapter 3

Reality

I wish I had known that heaven is all gladness, hell is all sadness, and we live somewhere in-between. Hell is all sorrow. There is not one bit of gladness there. But we are still living somewhere in-between. For years, that idea just didn't connect. Our lives will have gladness and sorrow in them.

I believe your life will change once you get saved and begin to stand on the Word of God. I believe in the victorious life, but until we get to heaven, it's not going to be all gladness. I used to think if you weren't glad 24 hours a day, 7 days a week, you had missed it somewhere.

Now, I am not a doom and gloom preacher, but I will tell you that stuff happens. Things are going to happen. You can have a degree of heaven here on earth if you know who you are in Christ, and if you know the truth of the Bible. Even the most victorious life is no match to life in heaven. We don't really understand the perfection of heaven. The Bible says you can't even comprehend or understand what God has laid up for us.

I thought that anything negative or uncomfortable was from Satan. I rebuked it. I rebuked a lot of things that I should have learned from. **What you rebuke, you cannot learn from.** It took some time to learn that some things are put in our way to call forth courage and faith. They are not placed there to stop you. God is not trying to stop anybody. But we live on this earth, and there are things we have to go through.

I got the revelation of this principle when we fought to get property so we could build our church building. What we had to go through to get our property! We were turned down for the first plot of land we tried to buy. We began rebuking the devil. Then we were turned down again for the second piece of property we tried to buy. We were turned down the third time we tried to buy property.

Now, it's very easy to get discouraged after three or four years of lawyers, meetings, board meetings, and planning, only to present everything and have the whole neighborhood turn against you. We were rebuking and rebuking. The fourth time, we were finally accepted to buy land. We tried to buy 5 acres. It fell through. Then again with a 9 acre plot. It fell through again with a 22 acre piece of property. But we ended up with 51 acres! We will soon sell a small portion of our land for a great deal more than we paid for it, and be debt free. I just didn't understand. I was rebuking these things, and God was trying to get something bigger and better into our hands.

I didn't give any credit to experience as a teacher. I was still convinced that I just needed to learn the Word, without having to have any uncomfortable experiences. Then I saw that these experiences taught me the Word of God. Now I know what Paul was talking about. I know how to be hungry. I know how to be full. I know how to be well clothed. I know how to be naked. I know how to have everything. I know how to suffer. I just believed in the blessing part. I thought anything uncomfortable or negative could not be from God. Now I know how to fight.

A young man was replacing an old president of a bank. The old president was retiring. The young man came to him and said, "I'd be grateful for any advice you could give me as I take over this bank."

The old man said, "There are two words."

The young man said, "Wow! What are they?"

"Right decisions."

Expectantly, the young man continued, "That's good, but how does one make these right decisions?"

"One word," he said. "Experience."

Still puzzled the young man replied, "But how do you get that experience?"

"Two words," he answered. "Wrong decisions."

It's true. You make a lot of wrong decisions and realize that they were wrong. I missed that. I was deceived. I was like that young man who had all the knowledge and none of the experience.

You learn more by looking for an answer than you do from finding it. I have learned great things. I have had great revelations from the Word of God while I was going through the scriptures to find an answer to another question altogether.

If only I had known that heaven is all gladness, hell is all sorrow, and we live somewhere in-between, I would have suffered a lot less than I did.

I WISH I HAD KNOWN THAT BACK THEN.

Chapter 4

Timing

I wish I had known that there is a time to put on lion's skins, fox skins, and sheep skins. There are times when you need to be strong, like a lion. That's the time when you need to be tough, and say, "This is it, brother!" That's the time when you need to be uncompromising and set your face like flint. There are other times you need to be wise like a fox. When someone speaks with a crafty tongue, you need to listen with a cunning ear. There are also times when you need to put on the sheepskin and be meek and gentle. I wish I had known when to wear these three different skins.

Back then, I pretty much stayed dressed in the lion's skin. I was quick on the draw. I was always too quick to reach for my guns. I was always ready for a fight and ready to defend. Then I began to see the two sides of Jesus. He would jump and shout. He was loud. He whipped the moneychangers, got upset and turned over tables. But then He was gentle and calm. He didn't try to be everything to everybody. He understood there are different ways to react in different situations.

There are certain issues on which you cannot compromise. You have to stand firm like a rock and not be moved. When it comes to the principles in God's Word, you cannot compromise. But when it is a matter of taste, you learn to bend.

I didn't know how to compromise when it was a matter of individual taste. There are certain things one person likes and another one doesn't. Look at people's different ideas about colors and decorating, for instance. I once heard of a preacher who had the sanctuary of his church decorated with orange carpet and black wrought iron fixtures. He did this originally in the 70's, and at that time, it was fine. But 20 years later his church still had orange carpet. People started complaining. Committees were formed just to try to get the pastor's permission to allow some people to give money to pay to change the carpet. He wouldn't hear of it. People started leaving his church all because he wouldn't compromise. The Gospel doesn't change, but people do. You can't reach the kids today in the same way you could in the 50's. Clothes change. Hairstyles change. Music changes. You have to learn how to get along and flow with people. You have to bend like a tree's branches bend in the breeze. If they didn't bend, they would snap off every time there was a little wind. You don't compromise the principles of God's Word, but as you deal with people you will have to compromise.

A wise man will learn how to do that. Jesus said, "Be wise as the devil but be as harmless as doves."

Use your head on yourself and your heart on others. Don't treat everyone the same. The Bible says to treat some with grace and some with fear.

There are some people who respond best when they are spoken to directly. You need to say to them, "You'd better straighten up. We'll give you one more chance, and that's it. You're out of here." Others need to be treated more gently and encouraged.

Ecclesiastes chapter 3 says that there is a time for everything. There is a time to build up and a time to tear down. There is a time for war and a time for peace. The key is knowing the right time and acting accordingly. Pick your battles. Use the right strategy. Put on the right skin, and you'll win every time.

I WISH I HAD KNOWN THAT BACK THEN.

Chapter 5

The Law of the Farm

I wish I had known that we live by the law of the farm. You are not in charge of your life. You're in charge of your decisions. **Your decisions control your life.** You are in charge of your life in an indirect way. Every single decision you make has a harvest. You make a decision and you put God's universal law into effect.

We are not under Old Testament Law. We are not under "THE Law" in that sense. There are, however, laws we must live with:
- The royal law of love
- The law of faith
- The law of sacrifice
- The law of the farm
- Natural law

Let's look at natural law for a moment. For example, no matter how much we may not want to be under it, we are under natural law. Take gravity, for instance…you make the decision to step off the stairs and you make the decision to go down. You can talk and talk until you're blue in the face, but you will not go up. Gravity will pull you down.

After you've stepped out, **you cannot change the law of gravity**. That's where the law of the farm comes in. We make decisions, then try to change the harvest.

You will reap according to what you sow. The decisions you make have consequences you have to live with. If you choose the mountain road, **you choose the hills and curves of the road.** If you choose to plant at the right time you will reap at the right time. Sure as there's winter, there will be spring, summer and fall. If you want food in the spring, you can't plant it in the summer.

I am 100% responsible for my decisions. You are responsible for **your** decisions. When I make a decision, I set a law in motion. God said, "I set before you life and death, blessings and curses; choose life. Please choose life so that you may live and be happy."

But you can choose death. Now, no one in his right mind would say, "Well, I'll choose death." But when you make a decision that leads to death, you have chosen death. When you choose the route you'll travel you're choosing the end of the road. **When you pick up one end of the stick, you pick up the other end, too.** One end may look really good, but that other side of the stick that's covered up by leaves may not look so good. The other end can be bad.

God doesn't tame with a whip; He tames with time. Retribution is time. You can sin and seem to get away with it. You seem to, but you're not going to get away with it. This messed up David's mind; he almost backslid because of it. He tried to figure it out, and he couldn't. He said, "I didn't understand how I could see people who did not love God, and did not act on His Word, and yet their lives were good and they prospered…. But then I went into the house of the Lord, and He showed me their end. Then I understood it" (Psalm 73).

We compare ourselves. We don't want to see the sinner prosper. We don't want to see them happy. The Bible says the way of the transgressor is hard. He's supposed to have a hard time. At times it may seem like they're not getting what they deserve, but time will get them. Time will always get you. You can have a good time, but after a while it will catch up with you. **Your decisions control your life.** That is the law of the farm. Start sowing the right decisions today!

I WISH I HAD KNOWN THAT BACK THEN.

Chapter 6

Weaknesses

If only I had known that you convince through your strengths and connect through your weaknesses. People want to know the real you. They want to see your human side. You may choose to call it your human side, or you may decide to call it your weakness. Whatever you call it, that is how people connect with you.

When I started out in the ministry, I never told any of my failures. I just told about my faith. I never told people I was kicked out of school. I would have never admitted that until about ten years ago. I would have never told anyone that. Who would want to go to a church with a pastor who was kicked out of school? But I finally realized that it would help someone to know. Being a success in spite of your weaknesses and failures gives others permission to do the same. Who knows? There may have been some man out there thinking, "Oh, God could never call me into the ministry because I got kicked out of school." But now that man has permission to succeed regardless of his past because he can see that I did it.

Some pastors have painted a portrait of themselves in which they seem perfect. They make themselves appear as if they don't make mistakes. I've heard pastors say that they have never buried a person. As long as they have pastored, they never had to conduct a funeral. That's all wonderful and nice, but people make mistakes. People are people. I'm around some of these men, and let me tell you, they put their britches on the same way everyone else does. They all have flaws. They all have feet of clay.

I didn't understand about connecting with people. Then I saw men who thought they had to be a superman. I saw them fail. Their followers were discouraged when they failed. So I decided to be real. I am not afraid to say I missed it, or to say I've failed. I am not afraid to say, "Forgive me." I can say, "I was wrong" or "I made a mistake." I can even say I don't know when I don't know the answer to a question.

You touch people through your human side. Do you remember in school learning about great men and women? Which ones did you like the most? More than likely, you loved and admired those who had to overcome something. We all love the Helen Kellers and the Sam Waltons of the world. Who wants to know about some guy who was born rich and smart and died rich and smart? We want to know about the ones who started on a shoestring and fought for their place in the world. We see their struggles, and it reminds us of our own struggles. We connect with them.

You can convince them with your strength. But once you move their heart, you then can move their hand. You move their hearts before you ask for a hand. Passion touches, and knowledge teaches. You instruct by reason, but you inspire by passion. Open up and connect with the people around you today. Be you, and be all you can be.

I WISH I HAD KNOWN THAT BACK THEN.

Chapter 7

Haste

I wish I had known that hate and haste are the passion of fools. As Christians, we do not hate people. It is fatal to hate. Nothing cheapens you more than to hate your superiors. Christians may not have a problem with hate, but most Christians are in a hurry and that is just about as bad.

Make haste slowly! When I began in the ministry, I hit the ground running. I thought I was ready to pastor a 10,000 member church. I was planning all these things we were going to do: build a huge building, have a big church staff, operate a large bus ministry, and speak at the biggest conventions. I thought I was ready to be "there." I thought I was ready to have and do everything the Copelands and Oral Roberts had and did. But I was not ready.

Before birth, there is always a process. There's always a period of development. **Very few things are created and perfected at the same time.** A woman carries a baby nine months before that baby is ready to come out into the world. If a baby is birthed too early, it can't survive. Even a mother wouldn't be able to take care of a tiny embryo that hasn't even developed lungs or a brain yet.

My dream wasn't ready to be birthed. I deserved what I had. I deserved a little storefront. I was in such a hurry, but I couldn't have handled 1,000 people, let alone 10,000. I couldn't handle those big bills, because it takes wisdom to handle finances. I didn't need a big staff. I wouldn't have known what to do with them. I was driving the few people I did have crazy anyway. I would have embarrassed myself speaking to so many people when I hadn't paid my dues yet.

You've got to pay your dues. **You deserve what you have right now.** Your dream needs a gestation period. It needs time to grow and to be fed. You will have to wait and take time to get anything worthwhile. It will come little by little. There is no such thing as overnight success. Thousands and thousands of hours of preparation are put into a successful moment. You get what you deserve. The cream always comes to the top no matter what size the bottle. If you deserve it, you will get it.

Progress has less to do with speed and more to do with direction. Good and haste seldom meet. Courage is a lot more than just standing up and speaking out. Courage is also what it takes to sit down, listen and be quiet. Courage is waiting for your time. If you are good, you'll make it to the top. The man who can wait has the mark of a great heart...

- Be loyal
- Be faithful

- Be hungry
- Grow
- Sow

Then you'll get what you want...
- Just wait
- Stay hungry
- Keep your seed in the ground.

There are times when it looks like it's just not working. There will always be a time when it looks like the Word of God is not working with tithing, giving, and sowing. If you have a heart strong enough to wait, it will work. Pay your vows. God's Word works. There will be times when it seems like nothing is happening. There are seasons just to be still. There are seasons to shut up and sit down and listen. Then there are seasons to stand up and speak. Wisdom discerns what season you are in. It will take more courage to be still than to act. It takes more courage to shut up and wait than it does to get up. Work hard, but don't force things to happen. They may not be ready to happen just yet.

I WISH I HAD KNOWN THAT BACK THEN.

Chapter 8

Substance

I wish I had known that some people have the entrance of a palace and the contents of a hut. Twenty-five years ago I didn't know this partially because I really didn't know a lot of people, but there are some people that have the entrance of a palace and the contents of a hut. Have you ever met a person, and after the greeting, the conversation is over? That's because there is nothing on the inside of them that makes you want to stay. It's all appearance. It's all on the outside, but like a gold-plated chain, after a little bit of time you begin to see that there's nothing worthwhile on the inside. Sometimes you find the appearance of something great, but there is no substance on the inside.

Before I met a lot of people like this, I thought you could get by with personality, charm, and wit. Then I began to wonder, "Is it really all about charisma?"

You know, we don't need wit, charm, and all that jazz. It's what is on the inside that will make people want to stay. It's not just **how** you say it.

It's **what** you say. You may be able to fill the seats a couple of months with a big show, and emotions, but if you want people to stay, you have to feed them some substance. If you're going to keep talking, you'd better be saying something, or people won't stay.

Some people have that appearance of the great palace, but you get to know them, and you find they are empty on the inside. They have nothing on the inside. Many times we admire a person until we meet them. On the other hand, some of the plainest and most simple men have treasuries of wisdom and experience just waiting to be discovered. Look around, and you'll find those people.

If only I had known then that some people have the entrance to a palace and the contents of a hut, I wouldn't have spent so much time looking at charm and personality.

I WISH I HAD KNOWN THAT BACK THEN.

Chapter 9

Staff

I wish I had known that wise men surround themselves with men of understanding who protect them from the dangers of the ignorant. A good staff protects a pastor from the ignorant. You need to see out of more eyes than just your own. You need more than better eyes…you need other eyes to watch out for you, and you need other eyes to give you a different perspective. A staff must be discerning. I have to protect myself, and I understand that. Part of the way that a warrior protects himself is using a shield. My staff is my shield.

Tiger Woods could get his own clubs when he's playing a round of golf. He's a big boy. He can carry or pull his own bag. He understands what clubs to use. He doesn't mess with that, though. He has a caddie to protect him and to watch over him. His caddie makes it possible for him to keep his eye on the ball and continue thinking about the next shot without having to think about what club he should use. The caddie determines the club. Occasionally, you may see them have a debate and the caddie will go get a different club, but normally the caddie knows the course better than the player knows the course.

Wise men surround themselves with men of understanding to protect them from fools. I can't see everything. I need eyes around me. Wisdom sees through the eyes of others just as he sees through his own eyes. With wisdom, I see through the eyes of my wife, my assistant pastor, my youth pastor, and my administrators. I depend on them to know what's going on and bring important things to me. They have to discern what I need to know and what I don't need to know. They do a pretty good job protecting me and keeping me away from things that they can handle without me. They can handle a lot.

Every now and then something comes along that I need to deal with. They bring it to me, and I appreciate that. They keep me free. I am a free pastor. I have got it made. I almost feel embarrassed sometimes. Someone asked John Osteen, "Man, how do you pastor such a big church? How do you do it?"

John said, "Oh man, the bigger it gets, the easier it gets. I don't do anything. I go into the office one day a week, walk around, look around, and then I go to the TV station, look around and do my TV programs."

He did those things, but now he's got people doing things for him. They are doing things for him because they feel his heart. My staff has my vision. They feel my heart. They are here for a greater cause than just themselves. I know they're not here for the money. They respect and love God.

I must have people around me like that. You are only as good as the people you have around you.

They cover my ignorance. I need people to say, "Have you thought about this or that?" I staff my weaknesses. I don't know about computers. I'm practically computer illiterate. I know very little about bookkeeping. That's why I have the experts doing it.

Protect yourself. Surround yourself with men of understanding who protect you from the dangers of the ignorant. I believe that every pastor over 50 years old should have someone run his church for him. He should be dreaming, studying, planning, and mentoring.

I WISH I HAD KNOWN THAT BACK THEN.

Chapter 10

Battles

I wish I had known that you have to fight many battles more than once to win them. I am a faith man. I am from the Tulsa group. I was raised on the teaching you believe and you receive, and that's it. You never mess with it again. You pray once. Smith Wigglesworth said, "If you pray seven times for any one thing, you prayed six times in unbelief."

Many people read that, and think I pray one time. I believe; I receive. That's it. Well, I believe there's a lot of truth in that. You have to receive every time you pray. But I began to see that some battles do not go away so easily. There are a few battles I have been fighting since I began in the ministry. I have been fighting a battle for my daughter Tammy ever since she was born. I can't say we haven't won it. She is much better than she was. She was born severely retarded. She's 40 years old now. From the time she was six months she started doing strange things. At first we thought, "Well, she's a baby, and babies do funny things."

But something wasn't right. She kept on doing it. We finally took her to a doctor. They checked her. She went through a series of tests, and we found out that she had three types of epilepsy. We didn't know what to do. We weren't saved. We thought maybe God was getting us. Honestly, I can't even say I thought that much about God. I didn't even believe in God. I thought we were just unlucky, nothing more.

Anyway, we got saved, and we began standing on the Word of God. They said she would always be an epileptic and a vegetable. I remember Mary coming home from the doctor and saying that they said she wasn't going to be able to take care of herself. I could see her being tied to the bed. She was just getting worse and worse. She had three different kinds of seizures, and they were very severe. She had supernatural strength. She could turn over the furniture in her room. She'd break glass sliding doors with her head. She'd bang her head on concrete. We had to get her a special helmet. She was pretty violent. She could do whatever she wanted to do at seven or eight years old. She couldn't communicate. We had to put her in a home. We've been fighting the devil for 33 years now.

I'd love to tell you that we've won. We have been chipping away at the mountain. Every time I pray, I thank the Lord that He is Tammy's El Shaddai. I declare He is her healer in the name of Jesus. I thank the Lord for giving her joy and happiness.

That girl is happy. She has joy. She is doing things they never thought she would be able to do. She goes to school. She has a job. We see her all the time and she is as happy as can be. She comes home, and she is ready to go back. She doesn't even want to come home. She has her family there. She knows us. She loves us. She does things they said she'd never do.

There are a lot of preachers who wouldn't tell you that. I preach a sermon called "Seven of My Greatest Problems." I just shared some of the biggest problems I ever had. I preached how I faced them, and how I overcame them. Tammy was one of my seven problems. I had more people come up and say, "Pastor, thank you. You don't know how that helped me."

Preachers like to make it look like everything's great. They live a victorious life. They can paint a picture sometimes, as if everything is fine and they've never been through anything.

I wish I could say, "Okay. Just speak to the mountain, and it's gone." I believe that when you speak to the mountain it will be removed. The Bible says that. But there are some mountains you chip away at. It gets better and better. You chip away, and you keep standing. **There are some giants you have to fight all your life.** There are not many. But there are some.

I felt that something was wrong with my faith because of Tammy. I took her to Burny Davis. He has gone to be with the Lord now, but he had a great miracle ministry. He was the Billy Graham of Europe. He cast out all kinds of devils. I took my daughter to him. He looked at her and said, "She doesn't have a devil in her. Sorry, Sherman. It's something that mentally was out of order or damaged when she was born."

We cast the devil out anyway. I talked with him and he said, "I don't discern a devil here at all." I had felt that way, too. Some battles are fought more than once.

We were turned down three times to buy property. But we have it today. It took years to get here. It didn't happen overnight. On the fourth try the Lord gave us 50 acres. I rebuked the devil the first three times. I can see the Lord just smiling, and saying…"Well, keep on, son. Keep on trying. That's good, but I have something better for you."

I am glad it didn't go through the first time. I am glad they didn't approve us the second time. I am glad we failed the third time, because we ended up with a better location, and much more. We will be debt free this time next year.

Some battles last a lifetime. The harder the battle the sweeter the triumph. It's hard for faith people to understand this. When something is going on, they quit because they think they are messed up. They say, "I'm not like the pastor. He's supposed to be a faith person, so how could this person die, or how could that happen?"

Battles are good for you. There are no heroes without battles. Medals are not won on the parade ground; they're just displayed there. The medals are won in the trenches. If life is all easy, how can you experience bravery? You have to stand up to some things. If you are brave, you stand against the problem, you fight it, and when it appears that it is not working, you ask the Lord to show you if you're missing it somewhere, because God never misses it!

I WISH I HAD KNOWN THAT BACK THEN.

CHAPTER 11

Differences

I wish I had known that your difference is your point of significance. You are different than anyone else in the world, and your difference attracts people to you. What is it that makes you different from anyone else? It is your look or your mannerisms? You are different! Enjoy it! God created you uniquely. Since the beginning of time and until the end of the world, there will never be another you. God delights in that. He did it on purpose. God is going to use your point of difference.

We don't want to, but we need to celebrate our differences. Not just tolerate them, celebrate them. Do you remember being a teenager and trying so hard just to look like everyone else? So many people spend their whole lives trying to be like everyone else when God has created them wonderfully unique. Thank God we are not all the same.

Who would want to marry an exact replica of themselves? We all want someone a little different. Someone said, "A woman marries a man because he is different, and then she sets out right away to change him."

Be yourself. Be all you can be. Don't try to be someone else. I went through a stage where I tried to be like someone else. Somebody told me, "Boy, you sound just like Norvel Hayes."

So, years ago, when I began preaching, I would copy his mannerisms. I would do little things.... I walked like him. I began kind of stretching out my chin and saying, "Thank you, Jesus" just like him. It was easy to do. It's easy to imitate someone. But never forget, it is your difference that will cause you to succeed.

You'll need God's wisdom. You'll need to grow, but your difference will be your significance if you let God use it. God doesn't give out cookie-cutter brains. God doesn't pass out cookie-cutter visions or personalities, either. He never thought, "Oh, I'll just make 10,000 just like this."

Imagine what the world would be like if there were 10,000 Hudson Taylors. We'd all be running off to China to be missionaries. Who would stay home and reach people here? What if there were 10,000 Billy Grahams and no Kenneth Hagins? Everybody would be getting saved, but no one would be training the new converts and discipling them. That's why God has made us different and given us all different visions. It will take all of us and all of our dreams to fulfill God's will in the earth.

We are all different. We need to build on our differences. We accomplish so much more this way. Start today. Look around and see what your differences will do for the kingdom of God.

I WISH I HAD KNOWN THAT BACK THEN.

Chapter 12

Wisdom

I wish I had known the power of wisdom. I wish I would have known that wisdom is **the** principal thing. I read those scriptures, but I really didn't understand them. If you would have asked me what the principal thing was, I would have probably said wisdom, but I didn't really believe it. I just thought it was a principle. Miracles get you out, **but wisdom keeps you out.**

I believed miracles were the principal thing. That was what I really believed. **Miracles are exits, but wisdom is prevention.** There are painful things you can avoid in this life through wisdom. Walk in wisdom, and you don't have to experience those things. You're not going to avoid everything. You'll have some hurts. But there are so many things that someone else goes through and you can learn from them.

Success walks with wisdom. Wisdom is the dress of life. You can keep on trying to change your life, but if you are doing the wrong thing, your life will be just as messed up tomorrow. You can do the wrong thing the next day. Nothing will change until you stop, get some wisdom, and turn around.

A man walking down the wrong road doesn't need motivation to speed him up; he needs wisdom to turn him around.

Wisdom backed by courage makes a great person. A man without knowledge lives in a world of darkness. He is just stumbling through life. We know Hosea 4:6, "My people are destroyed for lack of knowledge." God said His people are held captive for lack of knowledge. They are held captive and destroyed — **not by Satan, but by lack of knowledge!**

I was into the power of knowledge. I knew about it. I had heard it from Rhema, but I was only interested in its power. I wanted to sound like I had a lot of knowledge, but I didn't desire knowledge for knowledge's sake. Then I discovered that talk is cheap. If someone speaks with a cunning mouth, you listen with a cunning ear. I've been around a lot of people that spoke with a cunning mouth and it didn't impress me.

A wise man believes little of what he hears. He isn't a skeptic, but he knows to believe very little of what he hears, especially when one person is talking about other people. A wise man studies men as much as he studies books. Be a studier of men. It will tell you wonderful things. Wisdom listens with a cunning ear. Even a rattlesnake warns before he bites. You just have to listen for his rattle.

I listen for the rattle when people speak to me. We all see the same things, **but we don't discern them equally.** We're all the same. We all see opportunities, but some don't see things that happen as opportunities. They see them as events.

The only job security is to have more wisdom tomorrow than you have today. We have to keep learning. **Wisdom** is knowing what to do next. **Skill** is knowing how to do it. **Virtue** is doing it. In the Bible, skill, understanding, knowledge, instruction, wisdom, virtue, and character are used differently. They all have different meanings:
- Wisdom is the law of God applied.
- Wisdom is thinking, What would God do next?
- Wisdom is applying the mind of God to your situation.

Acquire some wisdom and put a little power in your life today!

I WISH I HAD KNOWN THAT BACK THEN.

Chapter 13

No

I wish I had known to say "no" when I really felt a "no." There were many times when a brother or sister would come to me, wanting to start a ministry in the church or do something. I felt it just wasn't us, or part of our vision. It may have been a good thing for the folks down the street, but God hadn't spoken to me to do that. I didn't want to discourage a brother or sister. So I said, "Okay. Go ahead, and do that." I would raise the money and three months later it was over. I have raised money for so many things. I helped people with their visions, and three months later, the equipment we bought is sitting outside and not being used. I am not saying that God didn't want us to do those things, but the vision wasn't strong enough in us. The gas runs out. The fire dies. People move on to other jobs, and the vision just sits there. Don't do it unless there is a strong "yes" in you.

Stress comes from saying "no" when you should say "yes," or saying "yes" when you should say "no." Stress is trying to be someone you're not. Stress is saying "yes" when your gut says "no." I wish I would have understood that I didn't have to say "yes" to everything.

Young ministers starting a church think, "If it promotes the gospel, do it." You should do what's in the Word, but there are a lot of programs and methods of doing it that are not part of your assignment. Just follow your assignment. It is better to do one thing well than to do 50 things average.

A great rule of life is to know what to refuse. The "no" spoken in wisdom is esteemed more than the satisfaction of a "yes" spoken in haste. Many times we say "yes" for instant satisfaction and we should say "no." There is usually little pain on the front end of a "yes." The payoff is on the other end.

You don't excite people when you say "no." It will cost something to say "no." It's better to know how to refuse. Sometimes you say "no" by not saying anything. I asked my mentor something once and he didn't answer me. He just went on talking, and I said, "That's pretty good." I knew what he was doing. He didn't answer me; he just went on to something else. Don't do that every time, but that's just how you say "no." You don't answer "yes." Say "no" to a few things today, and save a lot of headaches tomorrow.

I WISH I HAD KNOWN THAT BACK THEN.

Chapter 14

Disloyalty

I wish I had known to instantly fire disloyalty. This one cost me dearly. You can do nothing with people who are disloyal. It's not the people you fire who give you the problems. It's the ones who stay on with you after they have been disloyal. When you leave a disloyal man in a position he will cause problems. A disloyal person doesn't have a character flaw; he has NO character! A man can be disloyal to you and repent, but that flaw is still in his character. I believe it takes a leader to split a church, a leader with a character flaw.

I have allowed disloyal people to come back into the ministry. It's happened to me. It caused a lot of pain. I have had people leave my church, rake me over the coals, and then come back and repent. I forgave them, reinstated their position, and they turned on me again. People can come back. They can repent. That's fine. I'll forgive. But that person needs to sit there for a couple of years and prove himself. No matter how much he is needed, don't give him back that position.

There are two ways to really know a person: marry him or hire him. Disloyalty is the chief sin of staff members and the church. When you touch a man of God, you are touching God. When you come against a man of God, you have come against God Himself. The Bible says that.

People don't realize that. You'll see these people who have just been disloyal, attacking the man of God. They don't really believe they're attacking God. They're in church worshipping, lifting up hands, but they are saying, "Who are you to say that to me? I am not giving you that authority over my life." They don't really believe the pastor is a man of God.

Paul treated disloyal people differently. Sometimes Paul said, "Forgive them, Lord." Then other times he'd say, "Repay them for what they did to me." Three different times in the Bible Paul named their names and said, "May God repay them for the harm they've caused me." What a strong man! He knew how to handle disloyalty.

Now, anyone can come up to me and speak to me. But when someone comes **at** me, I put up a defense. The Bible says never speak to an angry man. You can be faithful, but not loyal. I wish I had known the difference. You can be at church on time, work hard, pay your tithe...you are faithful, but when you talk about your boss behind his back you are not loyal! When disloyalty shows itself, get it out. Save yourself a lot of pain. Instantly fire disloyalty!

I WISH I HAD KNOWN THAT BACK THEN.

Chapter **15**

Diaries and Journals

I wish I had known to start a journal when I started my Christian walk. I wish I could look back on the night I was saved, and the weekend after, and the month after. I wish I could hear today what I was thinking and feeling my first year as a Christian. You don't have to do it every day, or every week, or even every month. You may do it once a year. Start a journal of your Christian walk. The Bible is proof that God believes in documenting things and putting them on paper; we need to do it as well.

I am not talking about notes. I am talking about you putting on paper how you personally see things. This is private. It is just for you. Only you'll read it and see it, but put it down on paper.

I advise every married couple that has children to do this. I advise you to start this practice today. You should write your children a letter on their birthday. Do it every year. Just write what they're doing, and how you feel: "You are so cute. You just turned three years old. Here's what you did last week...."

Do it every year. "Honey, you're 14 years old today. I just want you to know that you went through some hard things this year, but you are learning. You are growing. We're so proud of you. You're a good person. Mama and Daddy love you. You're so special to us. This is what happened to you this year...."

Save those letters. Don't even let them know that you wrote them. On their 21st birthday, hand them the letters. They'll keep them for the rest of their lives.

You want to leave something to go beyond your grave, something that outlives you. If you're in the ministry, sit down at the end of the year anniversary of your ministry and just detail what happened during that year. Don't just write what you're believing for in the next year of ministry. Write your challenges and your victories.

Start a journal today. It will be a treasure for many years to come.

I WISH I HAD KNOWN THAT BACK THEN.

Chapter 16

Mentorship

I wish I had known the power of mentorship. A piece of gold isn't worth anything at the bottom of the sea. It's useless and worthless if it is lying on the floor of the sea. **It takes mentorship to bring it up.** You have gold inside of you. You have gifts, talents and abilities lying dormant inside of you. Your mentor will draw them out of you. That gold is only going to come out through mentorship.

Your mentor is like the fairy godmother in the story of Cinderella. The fairy godmother saw through the rags, the dirt, and the smut. She saw what Cinderella was capable of becoming. Everyone else saw a little bitty servant girl. The fairy godmother saw a princess.

Mentorship:
- **Is your ticket to the ball.**
- **Opens the toolbox for you.**
- **Sharpens the tool you are using.**
- **Is fuel for your success.**

Your Mentor's:
- **Hindsight is your foresight.**
- **Suggestions are your commands.**
- **Wisdom sees your enemy before you do.**

Understand the power of mentorship. Get yourself a mentor today! It's your shortcut to success. There is a special traffic lane in most big cities, only for those traveling with someone. It's called a carpool lane. You get to your destination faster in that lane. I call it the mentoring lane.

I WISH I HAD KNOWN THAT BACK THEN.

Chapter 17

Respond

I wish I had known how to respond instead of react. There is a big difference between reacting and responding. I used to do a lot of reacting. I wish I would have learned to wait 24 hours before I responded. I wish I had learned to settle down. Reacting comes from your emotions. Responding is answering with the wisdom of God.

I remember when I had my radio ministry. One day I was teaching something and I mentioned Solomon. Well, this little lady got it in her mind that Solomon was a wicked man. She wrote me a letter. She just chewed me up one side and down the other. She had never met me and had never sent money to me, or supported our ministry in any way. I got all worked up and said, "I'll show this woman."

I sat down and wrote to her. I spent about an hour writing her. And, right in the middle of it, I thought, "What am I doing? Why am I giving this woman, whom I've never seen before and will never see again, all this time? Why don't I spend this time writing thank you notes to people who believe in me? I won't change her mind. It'll just make her mad again, and she'll write me another letter."

So I decided not to mess with it. I threw the letter in the trashcan. I believe at that moment, I chose to respond instead of react. Responding saves your time and your energy. It brings or keeps peace in your life. Reacting is a waste of time and energy, and it only brings more strife into your life.

I had reached for the holster too quickly. I was quick on the draw back then. I burned some bridges I shouldn't have burned. You burn bridges when you react. You'll find that sometime later you may need to cross those bridges again.

Respond. Don't just react.

I WISH I HAD KNOWN THAT BACK THEN.

Chapter 18

Savings

I wish I had known to save 10% of my salary. It doesn't matter how much you make. You can save 10%. Pay yourself. Pay God, then pay yourself, and live on the rest. You should save at least 10%. You will find as you get older, you'll want to save more. It doesn't matter if you're struggling, or hardly even making it. Take 10% off the top and put it in the bank.

I know you can always use it. We were living week to week, and just barely getting by. When you're living that way, the last thing you think of is saving anything, unless you're very uncommon. I always thought we would save one day.

But "one day" is not one of the days of the week. You may think you have your whole life ahead of you, but time goes by quickly. It's amazing. I was a teeny bopper just a few years ago. Time is now. Life is what's happening while you are waiting for your future.

If you are a twin, and your twin starts saving at 20 years old, and you start saving the same amount that he saves, but you don't begin saving until you're 30, your twin will have twice as much as you by the time you both are 65. The interest he will collect with that ten-year head start will give him two times as much as you.

Someone asked Einstein, "What's the greatest thing you ever learned?" He said, "The miracle of compound interest."

Pay yourself ten percent of your salary. Force yourself to do it. Put it in an account. You'll be glad you did.

I WISH I HAD KNOWN THAT BACK THEN.

Chapter 19

Importance

I wish I had known to do the important, not the urgent. I did a lot of things according to someone else's agenda. Their lack of planning doesn't constitute an emergency for me. I wasted a lot of time counseling people who wanted my approval, not my advice. They wanted my ear, and not my tongue. I spent a lot of time with these people. Understand me, my office is open. I'll see anybody one time. But I used to spend hours and hours counseling them in my house, at their place, and just about everywhere. I did it because I felt I could really help them. I still do believe I can help, but you can't help someone who doesn't want help.

I believe the devil will steal from you if you let him. I know a lot of pastors who are really into counseling. I knew a pastor once who went back to school just to get his counseling degree. Maybe he needed the information, but he was a pastor, not a counselor. In a recent study, 246 leaders who had fallen into sexual problems were studied. They found that 90% of them got involved by counseling.

I believe a pastor over 50 years old shouldn't be doing any of the work of the ministry. He should be mentoring those under him. He should spend 90% of his time mentoring those under him. He shouldn't be doing the work of the ministry. As a matter of fact, no one in the five-fold ministry should be doing the work of the ministry. The Bible tells us that our work is to be in the Word. We are to pay attention to the Word and prayer, and that's it. The deacons were hired and brought on board to do the work of the ministry.

I wish I had known to do the important, and not the urgent. You do not want to open yourself to be moved by every wind. It may be fine for the brother down the street to be doing certain things, but don't open yourself up to every wind that comes by.

Someone said, "A fool makes much of what is little and little of what is much." It's very important that when you minister, you discern your time. Spend time on your strengths, doing what is important, and not necessarily doing the urgent.

Deal with the things that need to be dealt with. Don't just do something because something has to be done right now. If you allow your schedule to fit someone else's problems, the devil will just lead you from one problem to the next and get you moving in circles. Do what's important for you today. Don't live the agenda of others.

I WISH I HAD KNOWN THAT BACK THEN.

Chapter 20

Relationships

I wish I had known the power of relationships. Relationships will determine the length of your stay in leadership. Relationships will determine your success. When God gets ready to promote you, He'll send someone into your life. That's the truth. When the devil gets ready to demote you, he'll send someone into your life. Relationships will bring the greatest blessings or the biggest headaches you have ever had in your life.

Few men can do you good, but many can do you harm. Relationships are so important. Don't saddle yourself with fools.

God promotes through relationships, and the devil demotes through relationships. When we're infants, we need relationships (someone to take care of us). When we are old, we need relationships (someone to take care of us). You also need relationships in between. You entered this world through a relationship. You will enter the other world through a relationship, and what's in between you experience through relationships.

Life is like juggling five balls: work and finances, health, family, friends, and spirit. If you drop the work ball, it will bounce back. It's a rubber ball. If you drop any of the others, they will break. They are glass. If you make mistakes with your friends, family, or your health, you'll never be the same.

You can make mistakes in work. You can learn from them and go on. You'll be okay. We have to know what we have to keep up in the air, and what can fall and bounce back up. Understand the power of relationships and focus on one today.

I WISH I HAD KNOWN THAT BACK THEN.

Chapter 21

Price Tags

I wish I had known that there is a price tag on anything worthwhile. You have to pay a price for everything you want in this life. **It's always a price issue.** Whether you're paying with your time, your talent, or your treasure, you are always giving something up to get other things. I did not really know that I was paying the price in some areas. You have to be willing to pay the price for anything you don't have that you want. If you don't have it, you didn't want to pay the price for it.

I play the banjo. I remember I used to bring it into the church and pick and play. People used to come up to me and say, "Pastor, I sure wish I could play the banjo like you."

"You can," I'd tell them. "All it takes is practice."

Now, the truth is they really didn't want to play. They didn't want it badly enough. If they did they would have spent the time. When I learned, I spent hours practicing. That's what it takes.

Anything you don't have in your life, whether it's a big home, a big car, more knowledge, or more faith, is something you were not willing

to pay the price for. People just don't see it that way. I see now that you can have anything, if you're willing to pay the price for it. If it's wisdom you want, you just stay in the Word of God, day and night. You're going to have to give up other things, too; that is the price. I didn't understand that.

I paid a high price to start my ministry. It didn't only take my time and my strength; it took my family. My family had to pay the price, too. That's why you always have to know that you are willing to pay for what you want.

You can't stay where you are and go to another level. We have seen people come into the church, and they get to a certain level and just stay there. It's like their faith can go so far, and then they stop. They desire what we have, but they stay where they are.

You don't have to stay where you are. None of us do. That's the freedom God has given us. We can go on and become if we're willing to pay the price.

There is a price and a place. When you pay the price you can have the place. The amount of preparation determines the greatness of your place.

You will have to pay the price. It's a price issue. The price may be time. If you give your time, you will get what time will buy. Most want to do what I do, but not do what **I did**. A famous football coach said "Everybody wants to be on the champion team, but no one wants to come to the practice." Everybody wants to come to the banquet, but no one wants to do the dishes.

I WISH I HAD KNOWN THAT BACK THEN.

Chapter 22

Family

I wish I had known that the most important relationships are at home. When I started the ministry, I was so busy. That's understandable. I worked night and day. My family was involved. We spent "together time" building the church, but we didn't spend "together time" building our family. I didn't spend enough time with my children. I didn't understand my priorities. It is God first, then family, and then the church. I didn't understand that the church was third on the totem pole. I spent all my time and energy on the ministry.

I made a vow to my wife, Mary. I didn't make a vow to the church. God created me first before my ministry. God created the family before He created the church. In the Garden of Eden, God had a plan for families. God didn't have a plan for the church until the New Testament. I am not belittling the church at all. I think you'll barely make heaven if you're not part of the church. I believe in the church. I know how important it is to be part of the body of Christ.

But I made a vow to be Mary's husband as long as I lived. I did not promise that to the church. Mary loved me long before I was a pastor. She'd love me just the same if I quit being a pastor tomorrow. She is more important to me than the ministry — not Jesus.

The Lord made me a father to my children before He made me a pastor. It was so easy when I was younger to think that there was time. I thought, "I'll just get the church going, then I'll be able to take some time to be with the kids." But every day that passed was time I would never be able to make up with my children.

You can lie to yourself and tell yourself that you're being a good father because you are with your kids all the time. I spent hours cleaning up the church and stacking chairs with my son, Jimmy. We were always together doing stuff in the church. But that working together isn't the same as spending quality time together.

My son passed away. He was on-fire and serving the Lord when he died. As a matter of fact, he died on the mission field. We were blessed. He was a dear friend and a son to me. I am so thankful for the relationship we had, but how I wish I could go back to those days when he was younger and be with him more. Time passes so quickly.

There's a poem that talks about making the most of the time you have with the people you love. It says, "Send me the flowers while I live." It's so true. Don't let that time pass. No matter how good things are, you could always tell your wife or your child you love them one more time. You could always have one more heart-to-heart with them. The church will always be there. Problems and opportunities will always arise in your ministry life. Get your priorities straight. Start building great family relationships today.

Someone once said, "Success is when your children love you and your critics respect you." I believe that is true success. You can look in the mirror and see the role model your children are following. The most important relationships in your life are the ones you have at home. Success to me is seeing my wife and daughter make notes while I preach. Success is...those that know you the best still love and respect you.

I WISH I HAD KNOWN THAT BACK THEN.

Chapter 23

Risks

I wish I had known that you can never become a winner unless you are willing to walk over the edge. We want everything in life to be easy. We want things to come into our life just because we confess it. It's not that easy. We can't erase the consequences of disobedience and bad decisions just because we're positive.

It's hard sometimes to be positive. There is something inside some people that makes them want to be negative. I heard a story of this man. He was positive, but his natural bent was to be more a pessimist. It was natural for him to think kind of negative and just tell it like it is, but he chose to always be positive. His son asked him why he was so positive when he knew his nature was to be negative.

He said, "Son, I fight being negative every day, but I made a decision a long time ago that I was going to be positive."

You must be positive, but being positive is not a cure for lack of preparation. I went around saying, "I am healed." I was speaking the Word of God, but I ended up on the operating table because I would not do what was required of me to do. I was unwilling to pay the price of changing my diet and exercising. Many times I was confessing I was healed while I was walking around with a donut in my hand.

Now I exercise. I don't do it to lose weight. I do it for my health. I had to work on doing it just for my health. I was riding my bike just the other day, thanking the Lord that I could sweat. When you get to a point in your life when you don't know what it is to be able to sweat, you're in trouble. I couldn't break out in a sweat. I couldn't put forth that kind of energy. My heart was about to burst out of my chest whenever I had to exert even a little bit of energy. Angina was eating me up. But now I ride my bike. I work with weights. I am taking care of my body. When you're fifty, you have to be willing to make some trade-offs. It's going to cost you.

I didn't understand that you cannot be a winner unless you're willing to walk over the edge. You will find boldness to be the trait of every great leader. God uses all personalities, and all types. You might be a type A personality. You might be laid back and easy going. God will use you. God doesn't just use the flamboyant, but leaders take risks. They don't take chances. There's a difference between a risk and a chance. There are three rules for risk takers:

1. Prepare
2. Prepare
3. Prepare

You don't get profit without risk. You don't get experience without danger. You don't get a reward without work. Anything of value will cost you. There is an element of fear in some risks. I'm not talking about a bad kind of fear. It's not the fear that the devil is involved in, but there is an element of fear when you take a risk because you are going to a place you have never been before. Many times we want the profit without the bills.

I WISH I HAD KNOWN THAT BACK THEN.

Chapter 24

Trust

I wish I would have known to try before you trust. I didn't know that, and I put people in positions they hadn't earned. I placed them in before they were ready for the position. Not only did I hurt the church, I hurt myself and them in the process. There is a danger in promotion — **not being ready for it.** You're exposed to things, you see things, and things happen. If you're not ready for it, it will hurt you.

I gave some people authority, but they didn't have the wisdom that is necessary to operate in that kind of authority. I showed my own lack of wisdom by putting them in that position when they didn't have a lot of wisdom. Authority without wisdom is like a man with a heavy ax without a sharp edge. He's more apt to bruise people instead of polish people.

Treason and disloyalty are not character flaws; they are the absence of character. You have no character if you are disloyal. You don't have a character flaw if you commit treason. You don't have any substance or character in you in the first place. It's the cardinal sin as far as I am concerned. You can be forgiven for being disloyal, but that doesn't fix the problem. You are left forgiven, but void of conviction and character.

He who tells his secrets makes himself a slave. You can make yourself a slave to someone else by telling them things that you shouldn't be telling them. I am very careful, and the older I get, the more careful I am. I shared some things with my wife, and the next day she went shopping with a bunch of women. That's about as dangerous as a bunch of men getting together to talk about stuff. I called Mary and told her not to talk about the things I had shared with her. Of course, she didn't talk about it, because she has a lot of wisdom, and she's very discreet.

Our business is our business. It's church business. There's something inside every man that makes him want to share confidential information, but it's not right to do that. What good will it do? It won't do any good. Don't share problems with any one **unless they are part of the solution.** That's how you know if you are to share a problem with someone. Can they be part of the answer? If not, be quiet.

When people come to me, I tell them, "Okay. That's all I need to know. Don't tell me any more. It's not my business. You let them do what they do, and we'll do what we're supposed to do. Let's keep out of it." You have to force yourself, but it becomes easier when you make up your mind that you're not going to talk about people. Decide you're not going to do it. Just say, "I'm not going to let it become part of my problem."

David permitted disloyalty with his son, and he suffered greatly because of it. When you allow disloyalty, you're not just hurting yourself, or your ministry. You hurt the person who was disloyal as well. David allowed his sons to be disloyal. Brother killed brother. Brother raped sister. A baby died, and men died. There was so much tragedy because of this disloyalty.

It's a cancer. There are three characteristics of disloyal people:

1) **Most disloyal people will never change because it's a matter of the heart, not of the flesh.** We all have weaknesses in the flesh, but disloyalty is of the heart. Disloyal people want everyone else to change. They will not give anyone authority over them. I used to ask myself, "How can they do that when God says it clearly, over and over again, to be subject to your authorities? They will not give any man authority over them. Then they worship God, and they don't think they've done anything against God."

2) **They don't believe that they are wrong.** They think **you** are wrong. They never think they are wrong. They really believe it's **your** problem. They believe they have done everything correctly.

3) **They never pursue a solution to the problem.** You'll never see them instigate a solution to the problem. They think everyone else has the problems and should be responsible for fixing them.

Here are five ways to help you deal with disloyalty. They are simple, but they work:

1) **Do not lie about disloyalty**. Be honest about it. If a person is disloyal, don't try to make excuses for him. Don't keep giving him "another chance." Confront it and be honest about it.

2) **Make sure all your facts can be proven.** We volunteer together. We come together and work together and things happen. Even though we are Christians and we are set apart, things happen in close-knit organizations. Make sure it's not just gossip you are hearing. Believe very little about what you hear. You can hear the same incident described by three different people and get three different stories. It's the truth as each one sees it, but each one may leave some important parts out. Make sure all your facts can be proved. Gossip is not a fact. Good people have been destroyed because of gossip.
3) **Give the accused the right to talk and to explain himself.** Give him a chance to speak when you confront him.
4) **Ask questions.** Read actions, not lips. There's a lot more going on than just what's being spoken.
5) **Make sure you fire them.** It's as simple as that. Let them go. Give them all the pay that's coming to them. You'll avoid legal problems that way. Don't do it out of anger. Don't react. Just calmly let them go.

This is a hard thing for some people to learn. It has taken me a few times. It just happened again to me recently, but I believe that I have finally learned.

I WISH I HAD KNOWN THAT BACK THEN.

Chapter 25

Emotions

I wish I had known to make no promises when you are seized by joy and write no letters when you're seized by anger. Emotional highs can make us promise things we cannot do. I have felt the spirit of joy and made promises that I was not able to keep. There is only one thing as hard as going back and telling someone you cannot fulfill the promise you have made, and that is trying to keep a promise that you are incapable of keeping. People depend on your word, and it is so easy to think you are able to do things after you have tasted great success or a euphoric moment of joy.

I previously told the story of the woman who wrote me one time blasting me for bringing up Solomon on my radio program. She wrote me a two or three page letter, in pencil, about how lousy I was and how I shouldn't be on the radio. She said I shouldn't be a minister. I never met the woman. She lived across the state somewhere. I had never seen her before. She just happened to pick up my program on her radio one day.

I sat down to write her back, and I got about

halfway through the letter when I realized the letter wouldn't solve anything. She would still believe I was wrong. I would only make her mad again. I decided to take that time to write a supporter of my ministry.

If you ever catch yourself writing an angry letter, stop! Do not go through with it. Go ahead and chew it! Allow yourself to work through anger. Give yourself a little while, <u>but do not put anger in print!</u>

I WISH I HAD KNOWN THAT BACK THEN.

Chapter 26

Cost

I wish I had known what costs little is worth little. I gave a lot of things away to people. I used to give away my books. Now that I know how important a great library is, I wish I had never given those books away. If I had it to do over again, I would buy them the book. I would have never given away any book that meant something to me. I loaned out lots of books that I had never even written my name in. Then, when I asked for one of those books back, I never did get it back.

I gave a lot of things to people who really didn't deserve them. I gave away books and tapes without charging them. People who are not willing to pay for your years of work and discovery are not worthy of gaining your knowledge and wisdom. We have to charge something for a course or a seminar. It's not that we're trying to make money off of people, but it costs us to do these things. Prices go up; they don't come down.

A worker is worthy of his hire. I gave a lot of things away that I wish I hadn't. The people who sit in the free seats are always the first to hiss and boo. Realize that people who don't invest their time and treasure in you, yet still expect something from you, are the first ones to cause problems.

What we obtain too cheaply, we esteem too lightly. When you do not pay the price for something, it doesn't mean much to you. If you look back on your time in school or even in your career, the things you worked the hardest for were the most rewarding things. When you pay a price for it, it really belongs to you. It's yours. It feels good. You know it's worth something because you know the price you paid for it. Charging purges and qualifies. It also purges the freeloader, and qualifies those who are ready for your wisdom.

I WISH I HAD KNOWN THAT BACK THEN.

Chapter 27

※

Extremes

I wish I had known not to be too sweet, or you'll be eaten up; and not to be too bitter, or you'll be spit out. There is a fine line you have to walk in the ministry. You cannot go to the extreme. You cannot please everyone, and you cannot run over everyone. There is a danger in being too sweet. God called us to be as cunning as serpents. You cannot believe everyone. I have known ministers who were so sweet. They were sugary sweet. They were so tolerant, and so disposed to give everyone a fifth, sixth, and seventh chance. It was like they almost loved the devil himself. They seemed to be more of a politician than a prophet. You can love people. We're supposed to love people. But we have to love God more. The Bible never tells the pastor to love his people. We are told to love our wives, and love our neighbors as ourselves, but we are commissioned to feed our sheep and protect them from the wolves. If you don't take a stand and protect your congregation from the wolves, they will be eaten up. You will be, too. Those overly sweet ministers were eaten up. They lost their ministries.

On the other hand, you can't be too bitter. There is such a thing as being too hard. If you are bitter, people will not like you. People are vital. You need people to minister to. If you are too bitter, you'll be spit out. You may be preaching the best messages in the Western Hemisphere, but no one will receive it if you are too sour.

Learn to walk that fine line. It will save your ministry.

I WISH I HAD KNOWN THAT BACK THEN.

Chapter 28

Requests

I wish I had known that great men's requests are commands. I didn't realize that when one of my mentors was suggesting something, I should have treated it like a command. I'd be traveling around with Lester Sumrall, and as we were conversing, he would suggest a book, or a minister; I didn't take it as a command.

I let a lot of things past me. I would just forget, or I would think of it and not act on it. I regret it today. He wanted me to go to Australia with him, and I said, "I'll pray about it."

What did I need to pray about? We didn't have the money. You never have the money...there is always something else that it can be spent on. Money wasn't the issue. It did take a lot to get over there, but I could have spent 10 days with Lester Sumrall. That happened just a couple years before he went home to be with the Lord.

Imagine: I said, "Brother Sumrall, let me pray about it." I didn't pray about it. I went and I looked at our money and I said, "No. I can't go."

I should have gone. I wish I would have gone. I let that pass me by. I did learn a lot from him.

There was a lot more I could have learned. I just didn't understand the principle that great men's requests are commands. I am so glad I know that today! When my mentor says, "This is a good book," I buy it. He might not say, "Buy that book." I just pay attention. I listen for things like when he says, "I really learned a lot here."

I write things down. **Treat your mentors' requests as commands.** It's an important thing to understand.

I WISH I HAD KNOWN THAT BACK THEN.

Chapter 29

The Library

I wish I had known that the greatest minds that have ever lived await you at the library. I never used the library. I never went into bookstores. I'm in Barnes and Noble every week now. For me, the greatest gift I can get from anyone is a gift card for Barnes and Noble. I guarantee I will use it. There are some things in books that you don't want to know, but you have to sift through to find the information you need to pick up. You don't have to study about butterflies if you're not interested in them. They have a great reference department in Barnes and Noble. I told my assistant pastor one day, "I wish we had this in our church." I wish we had a whole aisle in our library or bookstore that just had all these incredible books that give you facts and information about men.

Never let finances stop you from being a reader and an information gatherer. If you cannot go into a bookstore and just buy things for a collection at home, start visiting the library. All you have to do is take in your license and fill out an application, and you get a free library card. The resources there are wonderful, too.

The men and women who have gone on before us left so much important information. They recorded so many of their experiences so that we could learn from them. The greatest minds that ever lived are waiting for you today. Get up and go enjoy a bookstore or the library today! You can do without eating for a day, <u>but not without reading.</u>

I WISH I HAD KNOWN THAT BACK THEN.

Chapter 30

Relax

I wish I had known to chill out. I wish I had known not to take life so seriously. I read an article about a 90-year-old lady. She said, "If I could live my life over, I would relax more. I would let up, especially with my children."

Another 93-year-old lady from Kentucky wrote, "I would take more trips. I would be sillier. I would take more chances. I would climb more mountains. I would swim more rivers. I would eat more ice cream and less beans. I would walk in the rain. I would perhaps have more actual troubles, but I'd have fewer imaginary ones."

I started flying kites a little too late, I think. I am glad I started, though. I am glad I got my red and white '56 Chevrolet convertible with fender skirts.

Learn to chill out. Have fun. Make memories with the ones you love the most. It's not about board meetings and famous people. It's about the people whose pictures you have on your desk. It's usually your family members who mean the most. The things you do with your family are the most fun and most important things you'll do in your life.

I used to have a golf cart. I would just ride around the property. I'd let the kids from our church and school take turns having a ride. Their laughter was a wonderful thing to me. It was just fun. Now I keep toys and candy in my office. The kids just love it. They all want to see me. I know how to have fun. I know how to relax. It has made life so much more fun and interesting for me.

Get a life. Relax a little. Let the top down. I will gather some children who are at the church and say, "Let's go fly a kite." I get it up about 500 feet and then I let little Katie hold the string. The look on her face — she's never done that before. Then I'd say "Go to the office and get a pair of scissors. We are going to cut the string." You talk about happy children. **Learn to look through the eyes of a child and you will see something new each day.**

I go cruising almost every weekend when the weather is nice. The top is down in my '56 Chevy. The music is playing, "In the Still of the Night." Cruising along, not a care in the world. Start chilling out today; you won't regret it.

I WISH I HAD KNOWN THAT BACK THEN.

Chapter 31

Perception

I wish I had known that baby kittens don't open their eyes until they're six days old, and some men don't open their eyes until they're 30 years old. Some men never open their eyes. They never realize the source of the problems they have. That means there are some people you just can't help. I didn't understand this. I thought I could help everybody. I had the Word. I had the Holy Spirit to give me insight, but some people never change. It was a great letdown when I realized that some people just flat won't let you help them.

Some men never see. I didn't understand it. **You can die in the land of milk and honey.** You can be there in the middle of all this abundance and prosperity and starve to death. You can be there in the land of milk and honey and die of hunger. There are some things you don't have because you won't reach for them. You won't reach for things when you're unteachable. The old adage is true. You can lead a horse to water, but you can't make him drink. Some men are unteachable, and you will never reach them. What you cannot reach, you cannot save.

Look for someone who has his eyes open. Start helping someone who is ready to change, and leave the people who won't change alone. You'll be glad you did.

I WISH I HAD KNOWN THAT BACK THEN.

Chapter 32

Criticism

I wish I had known how to handle criticism. It's easy to handle criticism when you know who you are. Jesus handled criticism well because He knew where He was from and where He was going.

I didn't understand that criticism comes easier than craftsmanship. I didn't know how to handle it. I didn't understand the people, even church people, will gladly believe and receive negative and evil reports. It is only a very uncommon man who will not receive negative reports. There is something inside of man that believes the worst in people and in situations. You might want to hear some juicy gossip about someone, but that doesn't make it right.

When people started talking and believing lies and half-truths about me, I didn't know what to do. People give pain to another because they are in pain themselves. It's hard to separate that when someone has said something bad about you. You don't realize that they are hurting. They have to be hurting with the pain they afflicted you with. It's usually the same pain they use to bruise others with. They hurt themselves. I didn't understand that these people talking about me were hurting people.

They didn't seem mean when they were loving me. They didn't seem mean when they were hugging my neck and telling me I was the greatest. Then, all of a sudden, I found out they were talking about me. Some people are like that. They love you one moment and hate you the next moment. I'd ask myself, "What did I do?"

I couldn't believe the person had done that to me. It's an emotional problem. Love is an emotion. Hate is an emotion. They really loved me. They really felt they loved me. They can make that emotion turn to hate. I couldn't figure out that it was all based on emotions.

Satan's information is free. It's easy to get. He'll give you something negative about anybody. God's information is not free. You have to dig for it. You have to search for it as if it was hidden treasure.

I didn't understand that we appear greater than we are. My best friend, missionary Jim Zirkle, gave me that thought about 10 years ago. I thought about it a lot and it is the truth. **We all appear to be on a greater level than we are.** When we hear someone, a special speaker, we are hearing their very best. When I travel somewhere, I give the very best that I am and that I can possibly do.

Learning to handle criticism is one of the most difficult lessons in life, especially when your life's work is helping people.

If you're out shooting dice and into prostitution and doing things wrong, you can expect criticism. You'll find that those that are always knocking you are on the outside looking in. Leaders are highly subject to criticism, because they stand apart from a crowd. The higher you go, the more you are observed...and the more you observe. When you stand out, the big bullets come.

The question is not "Will I be criticized?" The question is "How will I handle the criticism?" You will be criticized if you do anything worthwhile. That's why your enemies can make you wise.

It's better to be deceived by price than by men. If someone cheats you out of money, you can earn it back. But do not be deceived by men. We need to learn how to separate constructive and destructive criticism. Constructive criticism will build you up and help you. Destructive criticism is meant to tear you down. We need to divide it. We need to look at criticism, because there's usually an element of truth in what your critics say about you. There may be an element of truth, although they have the wrong spirit.

I've discovered that about myself. When someone criticizes me, there might be two percent that could be true and maybe eighty percent or ninety percent of it is wrong. There is usually an element, or a little bit of truth in there. If you're big, you'll stop and listen to it first.

That's what I try to do when someone criticizes me. **I try to separate the message from the messenger.** I don't shoot the messenger because I don't like the message he brings. I listen to the message. Is there any truth in what they're saying? Can I see a pattern in their lives? Is there a character trait that they have? Do they have a cheering section? Do they have a bunch of people standing with them? If it is more than one person, you need to listen. If one man calls you a jackass, don't pay him any attention. If twelve people call you a jackass, go buy a saddle.

You need to ask yourself, is this really true? One way of doing that is to ask someone close to you, who really loves you, "Is this true?" Don't confuse criticism with correction. There are times you need to be corrected, and God will send someone who knows how to do that. That's why we need to learn how to interpret criticism.

Someone once said, "Adverse criticism from a wise man is more than the enthusiastic approval of a fool." It hurts, because most people want approval, and not advice. We need to listen to both. Even good and honest people get criticized. Jesus was spotless, and He was called a drunken wino and demon-possessed. A person with a strong vision will not be understood by the crowd.

A man approached me one Sunday morning. "Are you the pastor of the church?"

"Yes, I am." "Is that your picture in the paper advertising your church?" "Yes, it is." "I don't like it. It's a bad picture." Now this man looked like he had slept beneath a bridge the night before. No teeth, hair not combed, etc. I thought, "Who are you to criticize me?" But I didn't say anything. Monday morning I was telling someone about this. I thought I ought to look at that picture. I couldn't believe it. I hated it! Who put this picture of me in an advertisement? The man was right. I repented for my attitude. I never saw him again, but my critic was right!

Criticism can help you learn to laugh at yourself, too. We need to be big enough to laugh and to admit when we really miss it.

I WISH I HAD KNOWN THAT BACK THEN.

Chapter 33

Humor

I wish I had learned to laugh at myself. We all do stupid things. There's a saying, "We're all stupid at least five minutes every day. The goal is not to exceed the limit." We all do things that are not very smart. We need to learn to have a sense of humor about it.

You can laugh off the little criticisms. There are so many things you can just laugh off. Maintain a good attitude while you're being criticized.

There's a story about a guy who was run out of town. The crowd was literally escorting him out of town. So the man got up in front of the whole crowd and he started acting like he was leading a parade. A poor attitude only reveals that the people who criticized you were right. Maintain a good attitude. Learn to listen. Learn to laugh at yourself.

The crisis of today becomes the joke of tomorrow. You know it's true. There are things that happened yesterday. They were serious things. You sure didn't laugh at them then, but you can laugh at them today.

Lighten up a little bit. Learn to listen to your critics and learn to laugh at yourself.

Remember...**FUN keeps you human!**

I WISH I HAD KNOWN THAT BACK THEN.

Chapter 34

Hurts

I wish I had learned that you may forget what you have done, but people you have hurt will never forget. When you believe in tough love, you need a lot of wisdom. When it's kind of your nature to use tough love, you'd better use wisdom. I believe in tough love when it comes to my children. I made some mistakes with my son.

There are some things you do that people will never forget. There are things that were done and said to me that I will never forget. There are some things my father said to me that I'll never forget. I will take them to my grave. There aren't many things, but there are a few little things that my father said to me. I know exactly how old I was. I know the car I was sitting in. I know the year it was, and I know exactly what he said.

There are some things you can do that will hurt someone, and they will never forget it. There are a lot of people with hurts that are self-inflicted. Most of our hurt is self-inflicted. We allow ourselves to be hurt. We allow it to happen. We shouldn't do that. I'm not talking about self-inflicted pain.

If you step on someone's flesh or you brush against someone's pain, it hurts them, and they can hate you. If I have a little splinter in my thumb and it's infected and bothered, even though the rest of my body feels fine, someone can bump into that splinter, and hurt my body all over. I can get mad at someone for bumping my splinter. It wasn't their fault that I had a splinter. It was in my flesh, not their flesh.

We may forget what we have done, but the people we have hurt never will. I realize in the position that I am in I could destroy some people. I could take the Word of God and destroy someone. Often, saints waste time fighting battles. A big dog can whip a skunk, but it doesn't matter. A hurt skunk will still leave an awful smell.

We have to grow up and not waste our time fighting battles that are none of our business. We need to remember that we can inflict more pain on a hurting person.

I WISH I HAD KNOWN THAT BACK THEN.

Chapter 35

Health

I wish I had learned to take care of my body. As ministers, we can get so caught up in the spiritual and mental, and forget all about taking care of our temple. If we don't take care of our bodies, where will we live? Sure, we're headed to heaven, but what about the here and now? We Pentecostals have undervalued our bodies. We downplay them.

Have you ever noticed that no one cares about your health but you? People will give you cookies and cake. They'll love you and feed you cake. It doesn't occur to most people to be conscious of other people's health issues.

I remember when Mike Murdock stopped eating meat. I took him to this place where they had great steaks. I said, "Man, they have the best steaks..."

"I don't eat meat," Mike told me.

"But they have the best steaks."

So he told me again, "I don't eat meat."

People don't care for your health. You need to realize that they don't care. They love you. They really do, but they just don't think about your health. No one will ever take care of your body for you. I wish I had known that. The only one who can do anything about your health is you!

This is very spiritual. If you are dead, what good are you? What good is all the wisdom in the world? What good is all the teaching you have heard? What good is your ministry? It will all be worthless if you die before your time.

Let's talk about this "When it's your time to go" philosophy. Many times the Bible talks about adding years to your life. There was a king who added years to his life. Ecclesiastes 7:17 even asks, "Why should you die before your time?"

There are so many scriptures (Proverbs 3:16, 3:2) that clearly state that you decide the length of life. It's your decision. You have to do things to set health in motion. When you're young, you think you'll live forever. But I have news for you. You won't live forever. You have to start thinking about taking care of your body while you're young. I didn't do that and it caught up with me. I ended up on an operating table.

Someone said the best passion is compassion and the best wealth is health. You can't buy your health. Hard luck is the punishment of fools. I know there are exceptions. We all have heard of the 99-year-old who smoked cigars and drank whiskey every day. You can be a fool. You can take the chance of being that one exception. But wouldn't it be better to base your life on the Word of God, and not on exception? That's called gambling.

Proverbs 18:9 says, "If a man does not use his own power or endeavors to take care of his body, he is a brother to him that commits suicide." So, if you don't choose to take care of your body, you're just as bad off as someone who commits suicide.

Look at 1 Corinthians 6:19: "Do you not know that **your body** is the temple of the Holy Spirit who is in you, whom you have from God. You are not your own." In verse 20 it continues, "You were bought with a price. Therefore glorify God with your body and in your spirit, which are God's." Our body doesn't even belong to us anymore. We gave it to the Lord. I wonder if we fully understand what it means to be born again. It's so much more than being nice and going to church. That really has nothing to do with it. It means giving your life to Jesus. You are giving Him your body. You are giving Him your spirit. Many of us have given Him our spirits, but we haven't given Him our bodies. Not just our spirits were bought with a price. Our bodies were bought with a price.

There is something I finally got hold of. Do we honor God with our bodies? How do we honor the Lord with our bodies? We can glorify Him in where we take our bodies. We shouldn't expose our bodies to sin. We don't take it to bars and places of temptation. The body will react to things around it.

Your body is not saved. It does react. Your flesh is stronger than any devil. Be careful where you take it. Be careful what you put inside it.

Honoring God is exercising. I changed my attitude about exercise. I exercise five times a week with weights. Everything I did like that before was to lose weight. That's pretty vain. Now I do it for my health. I thank the Lord every time I sweat now. I have to take care of my body.

Being positive does not replace exercise. Being optimistic is not an excuse for lack of care for God's temple. I believe in positive confession. I believe in the power of the tongue. You should speak good things about your health, but that is not enough. I was very positive about my health. I put down any negative thoughts I had under the Word of God. I spoke the Word over my body every day. I walked the floor claiming 1 Peter 2:24. I did it all right, but I ended up on the operating table.

Optimism is not an excuse for not doing. Optimism won't bend the laws of nature. I can climb a tower. I can jump off, and say, "I won't die. I shall live." I will die!

Believing involves **actions.** It involves **doing.** Optimism is part of it, but it is not the whole. We try to use optimism to manipulate things. We need to recognize that empty positive confessions will not change things. Don't just say the right things, do the right things. I was saying the right thing, but I wasn't eating right. Now I know that I must do both. **Confession doesn't replace obedience!**

I WISH I HAD KNOWN THAT BACK THEN.

Chapter 36

Action

I wish I had known that it's better to have a flawed plan today than a perfect plan tomorrow. It's okay to do it second-class until it can be done first-class. We always did the best we could. That's all God expects.

The man that makes everything beautiful but still doesn't do his best is out of God's will. Remember that people are looking on the outside, but God is concerned with your heart. He knows what you are really giving and doing.

Whether it's in the offering plate or in your paycheck, a steady dime is better than a rare dollar. I've seen some people who refuse to work for $8 an hour because they were used to making $20 or $30 an hour. They get fired, and they can't find another job. A month passes and they still aren't working. Two, three, six months pass, and they turn into bums. They won't go down to McDonald's. They say that working for less than they made before is "belittling God's gift." That's just not true.

If you are in that situation, you need to work wherever you can work. Work for $5 an hour if you have to. Don't see yourself there for the rest of your life, but give God a chance to move on your behalf. Don't sit around doing nothing! Remember that Proverbs tells us a man who does not work does not deserve to eat. Work for that dime today. Quit waiting for that $20 an hour today.

Theodore Roosevelt said, "At any moment the best thing you can do is the right thing. The next best thing is the wrong thing. The worst thing is doing nothing at all." The worse thing you can do is to do nothing at all.

Making a wrong decision is not the worst thing. It's not making any decision! Even if it's wrong, do something. Act! Stop talking long enough to do something. I'd rather fail than not try at all. Some people try and live safely. You cannot live safely and win. Take a risk. Go out on a limb.

I WISH I HAD KNOWN THAT BACK THEN.

Chapter 37

Fashion

I wish I had known not to be old-fashioned in thought or fashion. There is a Jewish proverb that says, "When you buy cheap meat, you smell what you saved when it boils." That's the truth.

I remember when a highly successful businessman from my church came to me. We were good friends, and he was a leader. We were talking about this and that one day, and he said, "Pastor, don't be so cheap."

I was thinking, "I'm not cheap!" But I realized I was thinking cheap.

I remember when I once said, "Well, I'd never pay $7.95 for a shirt." That was a long time ago. I remember hearing my daddy say he'd never pay this or that. He said he'd never pay a certain price for a gallon of oil for heating the house. Sure enough, oil went up to that price, and he said, "That's it! I'm not paying. I said I wasn't going to pay it, and I'm not going to pay it." He had them take out the oil and put in electric heat.

I said, "It's going to cost you a lot more money. You know that?"

He said, "I know it, but I'm not paying that price for oil."

I am bent like that also. I remember telling Mary, "We'll never be able to afford that."

She would always tell me, "Don't say that."

I would say, "Yeah, but we're always going to have bills."

She would answer, "Don't say that."

I had to stop thinking and speaking that way. I am not bent toward just claiming things. Some people can easily say, "Yes sir. Praise God, we're going to have this, and we're going to have that. I can't afford it today, but one day we will have it." I am bent the other way. There's something in us that gladly receives negative stuff. We cannot be that way. We cannot be old-fashioned in our thoughts, because it flows into our actions.

We don't use clothes that are out of date, or buildings that are out of date. They become unusable. I want to be usable. I would look funny if I got up and preached dressed in the clothes that people wore in the 60's and 70's: bell bottoms and ruffled shirts. You'd take one look at me and say, "Where is this guy living?"

So we cannot live like yesterday. When we started the church, I paid $55 for my suits. I'd go down to the Woolworths, and they had a big rack of men's suits in the middle of the store. That was about all the men's clothing they had. They were all the same. They had a black one, a blue one, and a gray one. Every now and again they would have two suits for $100. They were three-piece suits. I would wait for the sale and go in and buy my two suits. There was nothing, absolutely nothing, wrong with that. You need the $5 haircut and you need the $50 haircut. You need the K-Mart and the Wal-Mart and you need the more expensive stores.

But as you grow, you find out that the expensive shoes sure feel good. They stay in style longer, and they feel good longer. You pay a little more. When you go to the cash register you feel under conviction almost, but you feel good when you put them on. When you got to the cash register with a shirt for $2 or $3 you feel good, but you feel lousy when you put it on. The color runs out of it. It gets threadbare, and it's gone soon.

I had to start thinking bigger. It's not about being better than anyone else. It's just about being your best. I don't compare myself with anybody. I just want to do something big for God. **Being cheap is an attitude!** There is a difference between saving money and being cheap. I wear expensive suits now. Sometimes I get them half price at a place. I do find the best and I find it at a good price. Every now and again, I have to pay full price. It's not very often, but I do that.

So, if you're cheap, it's an attitude that can flow over into your calling. It can hold you back from what God wants you to do. Don't be old-fashioned. We're in a new age today. Old clothes are replaced. I don't want to be replaced. I want to be up to date.

Excellence will intimidate you or it will motivate you. Some people come around a spirit of excellence and they are intimidated. I have had people tell me, "You know, I don't know if I could get along in this church. This church is just too nice."

I do not understand how someone could come to my church, and be overpowered. They should be inspired. I tell them, "Just relax. Let God be God, and let excellence motivate you."

Don't be a cheapskate. Start enjoying a new quality of life today.

I WISH I HAD KNOWN THAT BACK THEN.

Chapter 38

Life Stages

I wish I had known the three stages of life are the learn, the earn, and the return stage. Lester Sumrall taught me that. During all stages we are learning, but there is a learning stage. There is also an earning stage. There is going to be a time in your life when you earn most of your money. Then there's the returning stage. That's when you return back to others what you have learned. I don't think anyone over 50 years old in the ministry should be doing the detail work of the ministry. I tell pastors to get someone to run their church for them. Hire someone. Find the right person. Have checks and balances.

I know pastors who are doing everything from visiting the sick in the hospital to cleaning the toilets. I believe by 50, the pastor should be into mentoring, not doing the work of the ministry. He should be putting himself into people, and he should run the church through someone else.

Your life is divided into these three parts and each stage is preparation for the next. Learning prepares you for earning. Earning prepares you for returning.

When you get old, you should not be thinking of trying to live on your $1000 a month Social Security check! I am not going to cut back when I retire. I'm going to believe God. I am going to go ahead until I die. I am going to be growing.

We have to understand the seasons of life. You need to know what season you are in. Draw from where you are at. Settle down. Learn if you are in the learning stage and earn if you are in the earning stage. It will return one day.

See yourself moving on to your next stage. Seasons mean change. Summer changes into fall. Winter is going to change into spring. Man's responsibility is to discern the right time for the right action. There are actions that go with each season. There are things you do in the learning season that you won't do in the returning season. You need to discern. Wisdom comes in discerning what season you're in and you doing the right things in that season.

Ecclesiastes 3:1 tells us there is a time for everything. Understand that.

I WISH I HAD KNOWN THAT BACK THEN.

Chapter 39

Confrontation

I wish I had known that facts do not cease to be because they are ignored. I ignored the fact that something was wrong with my body. It didn't just go away because I ignored it. I had to face it. I had to fix it.

There are things that pop up in the church. They will not just go away. They do not cease to exist just because you don't pay any attention to them. There are many times you may be tempted not to confront. You need to ask yourself one question: are you holding back for your own personal comfort, or is it best for your organization that you hold back? Confrontation is not easy. It is hard.

No one likes to go to a brother or sister in Christ and say, "We've got to talk about something that is not right." A lot of times we don't confront because of the fear of rejection. People pleasers are apt to have this fear. Some people fear they're going to make matters worse. Some people avoid it because it brings on too much stress. They want to leave it alone, but we have to confront. It feels uncomfortable, but we have to do it.

A lot of times people use the excuse that the Bible says, "Love covers a multitude of sins." The literal translation of the Bible does not say that love "covers" a multitude of sins. It says love "prevents" a multitude of sins. You can't cover someone's sin. Cover it in the blood. That's the only thing that will do it. Love without Christ's blood is not enough.

I know people who are not Christians, yet they are loving. They have big hearts. Their sins are not covered because they love. Love will prevent a multitude of sins. Jesus said if you loved Him you would follow His commandments. That is one way that love can prevent sins.

There are times of fight and times of flight. Walk away from an angry man. I never speak to an angry man. I wait for him to cool down a little. Never pacify because of fear. Never be quiet for the sake of peace. There are times when you have to make a stand for what's right. Even when it's not in your backyard, you have to make a stand. Just because it doesn't directly involve you doesn't mean you don't stand up. If it's wrong, you need to stand up. There are times to sit down. You have to know the difference.

There is a saying: "The socialites came and I wasn't a socialite, so I did nothing. Then came the Jews. I wasn't a Jew, so I did nothing. Then came the black man. I wasn't black, so I did nothing. Then came abortion. I wasn't a woman, so I did nothing. Then came I, and no one stood up for me."

There is a fine line. We are not to be correcting everybody about everything. The question to ask is, "Will this accomplish anything?" If it can't, just leave it alone. That's a good way of knowing whether it's worth it or not.

There are a lot of things you'll find yourself confronting that you shouldn't be confronting. It's not worth it. I confronted my son about a lot of things. If I could do it over again, I would not do that. It was just not worth it. I was getting upset over nothing.

Don't ignore facts. Face them and deal with them. Confront what needs to be confronted.

I WISH I HAD KNOWN THAT BACK THEN.

Chapter 40

Prudence

I wish I had known to be slow to believe and slow to cherish. You believe God's Word quickly. You should hear the Word of God, and say, "I believe it." Also you should believe it when people share testimonies of the goodness of God. But be careful about everything else you hear. A wise man will believe about a third of what he hears and very little of what he sees. The older you get, the more you realize that.

Some Christians, especially Pentecostals, believe just about anything. I believe every Pentecostal has inside of himself a hunger for miracles. I do. I believe I was created in God's image. There is that thing in us that wants to see miracles. But if we're not careful, we'll always be turning something into a miracle. It's not right to do that.

Be careful not to believe people who flatter you too much. When I first started in the ministry, people would come and just gush out compliments. I thought those people would stick with me until I was home with Jesus. I thought that they just loved me so much, but then they turned on me. It was bad. I wondered what was wrong with them. They just changed.

People flatter you. **Excessive flattery is to be feared more than hate.** Flattery conceals, and hate exposes. If someone hates, you know it. You know exactly where you stand with them. Now it's okay for someone to flatter you. It's nice to hear, "That's a good looking suit," or "You're a good man." But I had people that came up to me after every service and just shower me in compliments. They had to kiss me on both cheeks. Every time they saw me they had to tell me I was the greatest pastor in the world. They are not with me today.

I began to see there is something inside each of these people. There is a pattern of behavior. They were ruled by emotions. I believe that they really loved me, but people who are controlled by their emotions can easily be swayed. Their love easily turned to hate. They hated me with that same feeling that they had when they loved me. Be wary of flattery.

Believe very little of what you hear. He who believes in the supernatural needs wisdom. We better have wisdom. We don't want to be deceived by man. Wise men study men. There have been many con artists and cons that have come along, and the Pentecostals just jumped on them. There was a woman going around with blood on her hands. Blood would come out of her palms. She'd hold meetings and hold her bleeding hands up and say, "Look, it's the Lord."

That wasn't God. You don't find that anywhere in the Bible. They asked Brother Sumrall about it. He answered, "Blood? Blood? The only blood I know about is the blood of Christ."

Then she started finding feathers. She claimed they were angel feathers. She filled up her meetings. Thousands and thousands would come. Willie George had a video that showed how she hid feathers on her body that she had taken from pillows.

We have to be careful. Don't just believe people when they say they saw an angel. You've heard the stories about people picking up hitchhikers who were talking to them and just disappeared. I just don't believe that.

There was a famous preacher from Africa. They drove this old man around in a limousine. He wouldn't fly anywhere, so he had a limo fixed up with a bed and everything. I saw the old man one night, and I knew something wasn't right. I just didn't feel right about him. He was doing all kinds of things that weren't in line with the Word of God. He was later exposed to be a fake.

We're too quickly convinced. The Bible tells us to "test the spirits." Sound judgment doesn't believe something hook, line and sinker. You can be deceived by people. We all want to see God move, and because of that, we accept everything.

Watch out for exaggeration. **Exaggeration is akin to lying.** It cheapens your judgment and taste. I watch out for people who are always saying, "This is a miracle...." Everything is not a miracle. You can't attribute everything to being a miracle. God doesn't want you to do that. God doesn't need your help. I believe that an understatement is better than an overstatement. Temper your estimate. God doesn't need you to exaggerate your testimonies. Just tell it like it is.

Think things out. Diligence quickly accomplishes what intelligence has thought out well. Remember to "make haste slowly." Don't receive everything you hear. When you believe something, make sure you have been slow to believe it.

I WISH I HAD KNOWN THAT BACK THEN.

Chapter 41

Masks

I wish I had known to beware of the clown. A clown camouflages with makeup. There are a lot of people who come into ministries who have covered themselves with masks. They think they're doing something for God. There are a lot of hurting, dysfunctional people disguised as clowns. They'll show up in every ministry.

People wear different masks to conceal who they really are. You can really waste your time on them. They are not going to change, and they're living outside of reality. They are bordering on the bizarre and ridiculous. One day a lady who worked in our tape department just fell on the floor and started kicking and screaming right there in the church. I thought, "What is wrong with that woman? Is she just having a bad hair day, or what?"

Well, I didn't fire her, and later she caused a lot of problems. She was hurting. She was dysfunctional, and she tried to disguise herself as if everything was all right. Everything was not fine. It came out. One way or another, it will come out.

When you see the clown, you never see the real man. He classes himself with the liar. Think about it. Some use wit to conceal their pain. They are using humor. I am no psychologist, but I am telling you, you'll meet these people. You're going to meet a lot of these people.

So wisdom ranks higher than wit. Wisdom sees the wit. Some people camouflage themselves as great lovers of people. You've seen these guys that pretend to love people, but they're really just hiding their pain.

Just be who you are. **Wisdom sees things whole.** This goes back to being slow to believe and slow to cherish. Don't be a skeptic. Don't be questioning and quizzing everybody. Wisdom accepts what is true, and it sees things whole.

There are some Christians in my hometown that have a bad reputation among pastors. They go from church to church. They will not dig deep enough to deal with the hurt and pain. What kills a skunk is the publicity it gives itself.

Beware of someone who knows everybody. Be kind and beware of the clown.

I WISH I HAD KNOWN THAT BACK THEN.

Chapter 42

Teamwork

I wish I had known the power of a team. I thought I was going to win the city from the pulpit. I didn't understand I was only as good as the people I brought around me.

I didn't understand the principle that states that we never hire above us. If you were a five, you would only hire fours and threes. If you were a six, you would only hire fours or fives. If you were an eight, you would only hire sevens and sixes. If you were a nine, you would never hire a ten. If you were a seven, you would never hire an eight. If you were a five, you would never hire a six. You are always going to hire below yourself. The better you are, the better employee you will get.

I began to see that the better I got, the more people I had to have around me. I realized I needed people who are growing, because you produce what you are. You do not create what you hope for. You do not create what you beg for. You create what you are. It's a law of life. Like produces like. Like attracts like. I didn't understand the power of the team. I thought it was all about Sunday morning. Then I began to realize that I needed to gather good people around me and train them.

John Maxwell once asked his congregations, "What drew you to my church?" Five percent said they were there because they were influenced by someone else. Ten percent said they were there because they were going through a crisis. Eighty-five percent said they were there because of leadership. People want to be led. They want answers. Leaders have answers, and leaders need a team to get that to the people.

I WISH I HAD KNOWN THAT BACK THEN.

Chapter 43

Change

I wish I had known about the power of changing. All personal breakthroughs begin with making a decision to change. You can only do that by changing a belief. You start by questioning it. I heard a man say one time, "You will be the same as you are today five years from now if you do not change." All personal breakthroughs begin with a change of belief. We try to change without changing a belief. It will not work. You will fall back to what you really believe.

It's the moment of decision that your future is shaped. How we think and how we feel are merely obstacles along the way. If you are committed, you will make a way. To be merely interested is a big difference than being committed. If you are committed, you will find a way. When you believe you give your brain an unquestionable command to act in a certain way.

How can you change what you feel? One word...FOCUS! What you focus on grows. What you continue to focus on, you will experience. Faith is to believe something that you cannot see. Belief forms habit. Habit creates. Habit is the best of servants or the worst of masters. The law of growth works hand in hand with the law of change. There is no growth without change.

What prevents us from making a change? **Belief!** What do you really believe?

I WISH I HAD KNOWN THAT BACK THEN.

YOUR LETTER IS VERY IMPORTANT TO ME

My dear friend,
    I believe in the power of good, the power of prayer, and the power of agreement. If you are facing spiritual needs or conflict in your life, write me. I will pray and agree with you for breakthrough. If you have any questions concerning this book, I will do my best to answer them. Keep on top and rising and I will see you at the top in Christ!
Sherman Owens

For More Information About Sherman Owens'
Seminar Speaking Engagements, Cassette Tapes and Videos,
Or For Additional Copies of

Ladder to the Top
Why Don't They Teach This In Bible school?
Help I'm A Faith Preacher and I need A Bypass
Sharpening Your Ax, Vol.1
What Is Your Yes?
The Force Of Passion
The Shortcut To Success
31 Days To Victory

Write the author at:

Sherman Owens
Victory Christian Family Center
8200 Bee Ridge Rd
Sarasota, Florida 34241
Email: sherman@victorychristian.com

Wisdom Books from Sherman Owens

Why Don't They Teach This In Bible School, Pastor Sherman Owens shares in this book 31 Master Secrets Rarely Discovered. This is not taught in Bible school. $7.95

Ladder To The Top will bring a smile to your face, a tear to your eye and a desire to your heart to start climbing the rungs of the ladder to the top. This book lays down scriptural principles for a successful climb. $7.95

Sharpening Your Ax, The separation between winners and losers is found in one word: preparation! Read this book and discover the principle of sharpening your ax. $5.00

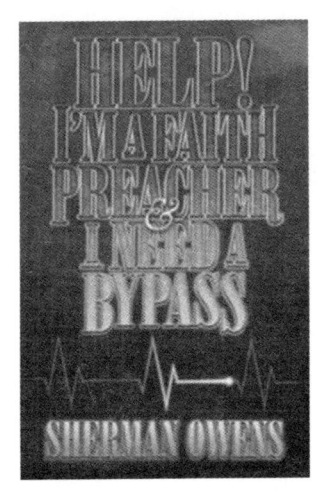

Help I'm A Faith Preacher and I Need A Bypass, this is the story of a faith preacher, who preaches healing and believes 1 Peter 2:24 *"by His stripes you were healed"*. But what went wrong? He needed a bypass. Was his preaching in vain? Why didn't God heal him? Did He? $7.95

What Is Your Yes? You have got to read this one! This will be one of the greatest discoveries of your life. You will be able to say "No" with a smile on your face.

The Force Of Passion, this could be the most overlooked ingredient for achievement! Passion is the fuel of possibility. You will understand how vital the force of passion is after reading this book. $7.95

The Shortcut to Success, mentorship is God's shortcut to success! This book will give you the insight to catapult yourself into God's future for you. $7.95

31 Days to Victory, it is possible that one of these secrets could stop a hundred heartaches in your life and bring a thousand days of joy. Sometimes the smallest key unlocks the greatest treasure. $7.95

MY CLOSING THOUGHT

If this book has blessed you I would love to hear from you!

You can order additional copies for a friend, life group, or a co-worker.

The greatest gift of all that you can give is the gift of wisdom.

Quantity price list for
What I Wish I Had Known 25 Years Ago

Quantity	Cost Each	Discount
1-9	$7.95	None
10-99	$6.36	20%
100-499	$5.57	30%
500-999	$4.77	40%
1,000-4,999	$3.98	50%
5,000-up	$3.18	60%

(Add 15% for shipping and handling)

Sherman Owens Ministries
8200 Bee Ridge Rd
Sarasota, Florida 34241

MESSAGES
BY SHERMAN OWENS

SEND TAPES TO:

Name: _____

Address: _____

City: _____ St: _____ Zip: _____

Phone: _____

Pastor's Name: _____

Please return form and payment to:

**Victory Christian Family Center
8200 Bee Ridge Road
Sarasota, FL 34241**

Or call: (941) 377-6401 Fax: (941) 371-7904
e-mail:sharpen@victorychristian.com

For Credit Card Orders:

CC#_____ Exp. Date: _____

Amount: $ _____ Signature:X _____

"Faith comes by hearing, and hearing by
the Word of God!"

SINGLES (Red-Hots)

TITLE	PRICE	QTY	TOTAL
3 VIEWS OF Jesus'	$5.00		
CAN A CHRISTIAN BE DEMON POSSESSED?	$5.00		
CONSPIRACY IN THE PALACE	$5.00		
GIFTS OF THE SPIRIT	$5.00		
HOW TO FORGIVE	$5.00		
HOW TO STILL YOUR STORM	$5.00		
ONE MORE NIGHT WITH THE FROGS	$5.00		
RIGHTEOUSNESS	$5.00		
STAND AND FIGHT	$5.00		
CROSS AND THE SERPENT (THE)	$5.00		
SEVEN MISTAKES OF LOT (THE)	$5.00		
TRANSFERENCE OF SPIRITS	$5.00		
WHO WILL ROLL AWAY THE STONE?	$5.00		

MASTERING MENTOR SECRETS SERIES

TITLE	PRICE	QTY	TOTAL
25 MASTER LEADERSHIP SECRETS OF Jesus'	$20.00		
SHORTCUT TO SUCCESS	$25.00		
STRETCH TO SUCCESS	$10.00		
THE UNCOMMON WORKER	$15.00		
THE VALUE OF A FRIEND	$10.00		
THINGS I WISH I HAD KNOWN 20 YEARS AGO	$30.00		
WHY WINNERS WIN	$10.00		
WISDOM	$20.00		

LEADERSHIP SERIES

TITLE	PRICE	QTY	TOTAL
6 QUALITIES OF A SUPER ACHIEVER	$10.00		
BORN TO LIVE LIKE EAGLES	$10.00		
GOD'S STRATEGY FOR SUCCESS	$25.00		
LADDER TO THE TOP	$20.00		
PASSION	$20.00		
POWER PACK FOR ACHIEVERS	$30.00		
VISION	$15.00		
WINNING IN LIFE	$25.00		
YES!	$20.00		

LEADERSHIP SERIES - SINGLES

TITLE	PRICE	QTY	TOTAL
DISCOVER YOUR "YES!'	$5.00		
EVEN EAGLES MUST BE KICKED OUT OF THE NEST	$5.00		
FREEDOM TO FALL, BUT NOT FAIL	$5.00		
HOW TO BEAT BLUE MONDAY	$5.00		
PROBLEMS	$5.00		
SALARY MAKERS VS SALARY TAKERS	$5.00		
SEVEN MISTAKES PEOPLE MAKE ABOUT MONEY	$5.00		
STRETCH TO SUCCESS	$5.00		
FOUR LEVELS OF RELATIONSHIPS	$5.00		

ALBUMS			
TITLE	PRICE	QTY	TOTAL
BLOOD COVENANT	$10.00		
HOW TO GROW YOURSELF	$15.00		
MISTAKES LEADERS MAKE	$10.00		
PAUL'S THORN	$15.00		
SEVEN BELIEFS THAT WILL TAKE YOU TO THE TOP	$10.00		
SIX I'D PICK FOR YOU	$30.00		
CLIMBING OUT OF YOUR RUT	$10.00		
SIIX I'D PICK FOR YOU VOL. 2	$30.00		
HOW TO GET THROUGH WHAT YOU ARE GOING THROUGH	$40.00		
LAW OF THE FARM	$10.00		
POSSESSING YOUR MIRACLE	$15.00		
PRAYER	$20.00		
SET YOUR BREAKTHROUGH INTO MOTION	$20.00		
HOW TO CHOOSE A UNCOMMON MATE	$15.00		
THE UNCOMMON MAN / THE UNCOMMON WOMAN	$15.00		
TRANSFERENCE OF SPIRITS	$10.00		
WHAT IS A GREAT CHURCH	$10.00		
WHY BAD THINGS HAPPEN TO GOOD PEOPLE	$10.00		
X-RATED SEX	$10.00		
YOUR DOOR OUT OF TROUBLE	$20.00		

BOOKS			
THE SHORTCUT TO SUCCESS	$7.95		
HELP! I'M A FAITH PREACHER & I NEED A BYPASS	$7.95		
LADDER TO THE TOP	$7.95		
WHAT IS YOUR YES?	$7.95		
WHY DON'T THEY TEACH THIS IN BIBLE SCHOOL?	$7.95		
SHARPENING YOUR AX (VOL 1)	$5.00		
THE FORCE OF PASSION	$7.95		
31 DAYS TO VICTORY	$5.00		

ORDER SUBTOTAL			
SHIPPING/HANDELING(Add 15% Per Order)			
Single Tapes (Each)	$0.75		
Books (Each)	$1.95		
TOTAL ENCLOSED			